The Chicago Black Hawks Story

The
Chicago
Black Hawks
Story

by

George Vass

FOLLETT PUBLISHING COMPANY
Chicago

Library of Congress Catalog Card Number: 69-15978

ISBN 0-695-80202-X Trade binding

First Printing J

Contents

1. The Last Shall Be First 1
2. Birth of the Black Hawks 9
3. Muldoon's Curse 14
4. Paddy's Legacy 18
5. The Age of Coaches 24
6. The Silver Age Begins 29
7. A "Shot" and a Goalie 36
8. Twenty-One Seconds to Glory 44
9. No Place To Go but Up 53
10. The Goal and Mr. Goalie 63
11. The Accursed 71
12. Stan the Man 79
13. The Scooter Line 103
14. The Look of a Goal 109
15. The Perfect Mesomorph 114
16. Not One Alone 134
17. The Tormentors 139
18. The Defenders 144
19. Man With a Goal 149
20. Decline and Fall 155
21. Ashes to Gold Dust 169
22. Tony Zero the Roamer 184
23. Maggie the Snowthrower 199
24. End of the Beginning 212
    The Black Hawks Through the Years 216

1

The Last Shall Be First

IT HAD been just a dream after all, and for a moment it vanished like smoke in the wind as with infinite grace and deceptive speed big Jean Beliveau of the Montreal Canadiens skated across the blue line, the puck cradled on his stick.

Beliveau had shattered the dreams of many anxious foes in his seventeen years as kingpin of the Canadiens. Now, once more, he loomed even taller than his imposing six feet three inches, as he bore down menacingly on Chicago goalie Tony Esposito, the Mr. Zero of the Black Hawks.

Esposito crouched expectantly in front of the cage of steel and rope that it was his task and torment to guard. He moved out slightly, trying to expand in every dimension as he awaited the instant the puck would come hurtling at him off Beliveau's stick.

But Beliveau, with the split-second decisiveness and flowing motion of experience under pressure, passed the puck to wing Yvan Cournoyer, who was flashing into the Hawk defensive zone at his side. Continuing his head-on rush, now without the puck, Beliveau drew Hawk defenseman Bill White with him toward the net and, at the last instant, swerved to skate parallel across the goal mouth. Timing the shot perfectly, Cournoyer backhanded the puck from 30 feet away. Esposito, screened by Beliveau and

White, lost sight of the puck as it flew into the upper corner of the net for a goal that gave the Canadiens a 1-0 lead midway in the first period.

The crowd of more than 20,000 fans who had gathered in Chicago Stadium to see the Black Hawks win a championship on April 5, 1970, collapsed into anguished silence. Perhaps it had been too much to hope, to dream the Hawks could win this game and so write a fairy tale ending to a story never matched in the National Hockey League and seldom equalled in any sport—the rise of a team from last place to first from one season to the next.

The Hawks had finished sixth, the lowest rung of the Eastern Division in the 1968-69 season. When the 1969-70 campaign started, few fans or "experts" gave them much chance of finishing as high as fourth place, the lowest position that would qualify them for the Stanley Cup play-offs. Certainly, no one had dreamed the Hawks would be playing the final game of the regular season on Sunday, April 5, with the assurance of finishing first by winning this last of 76 contests. Fewer yet would have imagined that the Canadiens, who had finished first the previous season and had won the Stanley Cup, would need a victory or tie in this final game to qualify for the play-offs.

Yet those were the stakes: A divisional title for the Black Hawks and either redemption or disgrace for the Canadiens, who had not missed the play-offs for 22 seasons. The Hawks went into the game tied for first place with the Boston Bruins, each team having 97 standing points. But the Hawks had more victories than the Bruins and would take the title on that basis if they beat Montreal even if Boston defeated Toronto that night to keep pace in points.

The Canadiens needed a victory, a tie, or at least five goals in defeat to edge the New York Rangers for fourth place. If they lost and scored less than five goals, Canada would be unrepresented in the Stanley Cup play-offs for the first time in history. Toronto already had been eliminated from contention. It was almost as much for flag and country as for the Canadiens that Beliveau and Cournoyer scored the goal that put Montreal ahead.

Yet these Hawks were seldom daunted when their opponent scored the first goal. Keith Magnuson, the flame-haired rookie defenseman, had noted that fact during the fierce drive that carried the Hawks from fifth place in late February to the top at the end of March.

"It seems that almost every game we've been giving up the first goal or two," said Magnuson wonderingly. "But even on the road when we've fallen behind 1-0 or 2-0 we've pulled together and caught the other guys. That has to be the mark of a good team, and the more often it has happened the more confident we've become that we could do it."

Yet there had to be worry, for the six minutes of tension that followed Cournoyer's goal, whether the Hawks could do it this time. They kept up a vigorous assault on Montreal goalie Rogatien Vachon without being able to get the puck past him. The little man with the long side-burns kicked aside, caught, or pounced on every shot that Bobby Hull, Stan Mikita, Pit Martin, and the others fired at him. Then along came Jim Pappin, the six-foot, dour-faced right wing on the Martin line, building up velocity as he shot down the right boards out of the Hawk zone after taking a pass from Magnuson. Two strides across the blue line and he swelled up with power and belted a slapshot that screamed into the net past Vachon's kicking left leg.

The game was tied 1-1 at 15:49 of the first period, and the crowd vented its relief and joy with an explosion of emotion that lifted the Hawks and restored their confidence. Now they were looking for the "break'" that would give them the lead. It came at 17:18 when a penalty was called on Canadien forward Jacques Lemaire.

Martin led the power-play rush. He shot across the blue line into the Canadien zone, circled to his left, and passed the puck to defenseman Doug Mohns at left point. Still moving, Martin faked Canadien defenseman J. C. Tremblay from his position at Vachon's left, then streaked toward the goal mouth. The puck came back to him from Mohns, and Martin smashed it past Vachon to put the Hawks ahead 2-1.

"All I could see was the space between the goalie and the net," Martin said later. "I had my eyes fixed on that space. I didn't even see the goalie—I had no idea of where he was or what he was doing. I just wanted to blast that puck into that space."

He did, and the Hawks had the 2-1 lead they carried into the second period until Bobby Hull made it 3-1 with a 30-foot slapshot at 1:24. However, there was little time to relax. Just two minutes later a shot by Beliveau eluded Esposito, and the Canadiens, behind just 3-2, were in the game again. The two teams sparred cautiously through the remainder of the second period, again waiting for the "break."

It came to the Hawks as Martin once again found himself alone in front of Vachon at 7:15 of the third period and slapped the puck past the goalie from 20 feet out. Just three minutes later Martin put in his third goal of the night to give the Hawks a 5-2 lead, and the roars of "We're No. 1! We're No. 1!" from the Stadium crowd rang in his ears as he jumped for joy on the ice littered with hats, the traditional salute to his "hat trick" of three goals.

Pappin, a grin splitting his often sad face, skated up to Martin.

"Hey, you've got the bonus for scoring 30 goals after all, you little so-and-so," Pappin yelled over the uproar.

"Geez, I hadn't thought of that," Martin yelled back. "That's right, I do. How about that! I do!"

Later, he explained: "When I got to the Stadium I wasn't even thinking about scoring 30 goals if I could score three tonight. I was just thinking about how we were going to play."

He must have been, for nobody could have played better than the little center did that night. His third goal killed the Canadiens, now trailing 5-2. Montreal coach Claude Ruel decided to forget about trying to win and to concentrate on getting the five goals needed to pass the Rangers for fourth place.

For the last 7½ minutes, each time Montreal gained possession of the puck, Ruel took goalie Vachon out to get an extra forward on the ice. Every time Vachon skated to the bench the Hawks got the puck and popped it into the empty net. It was a crescendo of frenzy, the fans screaming, "We're No. 1! We're No. 1!" again and again, littering the ice with cups and programs every time another goal was scored. Mercifully, the final buzzer sounded after Eric Nesterenko, Bobby Hull, Dennis Hull, Cliff Koroll, and Gerry Pinder each scored empty net goals to produce the end result: Hawks 10, Canadiens 2.

The fairy tale had come true as triumph and travesty. The Hawks, for the second time in their 44-year history, had finished first and won the Prince of Wales Cup.

Mikita and Lou Angotti hoisted Coach Billy Reay to their shoulders and carried him to center ice. Mikita led the crowd in a huge cheer for the coach who had guided the Hawks from sixth to first at a single bound, the same coach whom the crowd had booed so lustily just a year before.

And in the tumult and the chanting of "We're No. 1! We're No. 1!" over and over again, the echoes following their descent into the basement of the Stadium, the Hawks clumped into their locker room. Mikita held up a hand as the players prepared to uncork the champagne of champions: "Wait a minute. Let's kneel and say a little prayer." Thus a moment of silence, a quiet prayer of thanks for the wonder that had come to pass, preceded the riotous celebration that greeted the newspaper reporters and men of radio and TV who came into the locker room just a little while later. They saw Dennis Hull throw his arms around

Martin and hug him before each doused the other with champagne, the shampoo that crowns conquerors in sports.

"We did it! We did it!" yelled Martin and the words came echoing from Dennis, with the soft addition, "What a game you played! What a game you had!"

And they rocked in delight, the champagne dripping down their suspenders, with Martin's smooth face glowing with the joy of having scored three goals in probably the most satisfying victory in Hawk history.

"The greatest night I've ever had by far," he yelled. "Nothing like it ever."

No, not even the two four-goal nights he'd had in his seven-season career could touch this one. And it wasn't just because he had led the Hawks to the top, but for reasons beyond that.

Dennis Hull supplied one of those reasons:

"It was appropriate that Martin should be the hero tonight because it has been his line that has kept us going the last few weeks. He and Jim Pappin and Gerry Pinder have been getting the goals, making the big plays week after week. What a season he's had!"

He *had* had a great season, and it was fitting that he should, almost necessary, because he had put himself on the spot before it started. The summer before, after the Hawk's sad decline to sixth place, it was Martin who blasted the team as lacking in spirit, in being unwilling and uninterested in working together. He had criticized the management and Coach Reay for having one set of rules for the big stars such as Bobby Hull and Mikita and another for the ordinary players. Blunt and outspoken, Martin had put into words what others thought but did not dare to say.

"It wasn't a spur of the moment thing," he said on the night of victory. "I thought about it before I said it. Maybe it could have backfired on me if I'd had a bad season. Maybe it's fortunate that I did have a good one.

"But I knew when I said it that Billy Reay would respect

what I had to say. I think he's a man who knows who goes out there to work and who doesn't. I wasn't afraid that he was going to turn me off."

As Martin spoke, goalie Esposito, his bared shoulders and chest covered with purple and yellow bruises, slumped in his cubicle, just staring vacantly at the locker room ceiling. He didn't even seem aware of the wild celebration around him as the players sloshed champagne over each other and the newsmen. Esposito just sat and stared, exhausted completely, drained by the pressure of the final game and the long season, the great season. He had set a record for goalies with 15 shutouts and had won the Vezina Trophy for the Hawks. He had been more than human.

"There's the guy who has been the difference," said Martin, nodding at Tony. "He has made stops nobody could believe in game after game. He is the guy we've rallied around. I don't think there ever has been a goaltender with a season like the one he has had."

Probably not. And that, too, was fitting, because Esposito was technically a rookie, although he had played 13 games for Montreal the season before. And this Hawk triumph was that of the rookies, the youngsters Esposito, Pinder, Koroll, and Magnuson, who had appeared suddenly on the scene to transform a last-place team into a champion.

More than anything else it was this triumph of youth, of a rebuilt team that made it such a special night for Coach Reay. He had led the Hawks to their first Prince of Wales Cup three years before and had been on Montreal's Stanley Cup winning team as a player in his youth. But this new triumph was sweeter than any that had preceded it.

"This season has given me more satisfaction than any other. That's because we've had total effort from everybody all the time, which is what a coach works and hopes for but seldom gets.

"And to win with so many rookies! A lot of people figured these kids would collapse in the stretch, but they came on stronger and stronger as it went on. They were given a challenge and they rose to the opportunity, which has to give a coach great satisfaction.

"To think that we lost the first five games of the season and then came on to achieve this! It's unbelievable. We had to fight an uphill battle all the way. We had to play play-off hockey almost from the start. Nothing in my experience ever has matched this. This is the proudest moment of my life."

It was and it had to be. Nothing that happened to the Hawks subsequently could diminish that. Certainly, the young Hawks couldn't go on to win the Stanley Cup, although they took the quarterfinal series from the Detroit Red Wings in four straight games. Boston proved too strong for them in the semifinals, sweeping four games.

But after the final defeat of that series, a bitterly fought 5-4 victory by the Bruins at Boston, Reay summed up the essential valor of the 1969-70 season calmly, without a trace of bitterness:

"We have lost four straight play-off games and our season is over. But I'll tell you all—especially the experts who never thought we'd achieve the play-offs—that I'm tremendously proud of this hockey team, the way they worked, the way they tried, the way they fought all season.

"No team in my lifetime in hockey has given me the thrill that this team has."

It was a statement echoed by Hawks fans, many of whom turned out at O'Hare Field to welcome the team home after the final play-off game. The 1969-70 season was a highlight in Hawk history. And yet it was but the latest chapter in that history, which had its beginning almost half a century before.

It is a tale worth telling from the start.

2

Birth of the Black Hawks

QUEEN MARIE of Romania had a chance to see history in the making but failed to take advantage of it. She attended a luncheon of the Union League Club of Chicago on November 17, 1926, as part of her highly publicized tour of the United States. Many of the 2,000 club members and their guests who thronged to see Queen Marie had another engagement scheduled that evening. To make the day complete, they were going to attend a hockey game, the first ever played in Chicago by the Black Hawks. It would have been perfectly proper even for a queen to attend the game. It was to be as much a social event as a sporting match. Among those planning their evenings around the game were Marshall Field, of department store fame, and various Swifts and Armours, who had extracted high social position as well as everything but the squeal from pigs. Queen Marie would have known as much about hockey as most of those who were planning to attend the game—which was next to nothing.

Hockey was new and strange to most Chicagoans, although a few had seen games in Canada or while attending some of the posh eastern colleges that had teams. Most of the 9,000 people who streamed into Chicago Coliseum on the evening of November 17, 1926—not including

Queen Marie, who rejected the chance to go—never had seen hockey before. They turned out partly because of curiosity aroused by newspaper stories detailing preparations for the introduction of major league hockey to Chicago. And they came to contribute to charity as part of their social obligations. The Junior League and other charitable organizations were to share in the gate proceeds.

Nothing in those long-ago days could bring out the rich in greater numbers than the promise of a novelty, in this case an imported team game described in newspaper stories as being extremely fast and exciting—and also not too difficult to understand.

Sure, the stories coyly hinted at the violence of the game, but that made it only the more appetizing in an age in which boxing was second only to baseball in popularity. The ladies demurred just slightly before pretending to give in and accompany their husbands or boy friends to the Coliseum to see the much-advertised game between St. Patrick's of Toronto and the new Black Hawks.

It was like opening night at the opera. In fact, many of those who attended the hockey game had turned out the evening before to hear Rosa Raisa sing the title role in *Aida* at the Chicago Civic Opera, with Queen Marie also in attendance. They wore much the same clothes to the hockey game—and understood just about as much of what was going on.

Ice hockey was an almost unknown sport in most parts of the United States in 1926. The game had drifted southward from Canada at the turn of the century into New England, the Pacific Northwest and parts of the Upper Middle West. Teams were even formed at a few colleges, mostly in New England.

It was at these eastern colleges that several of the people who played a role in the founding of the Black Hawks had become familiar with the game. Most prominent among them was Major Frederic McLaughlin, whose fortune was derived from the coffee industry. The major was a sportsman of some repute. He was considered one of the finest polo players in the Middle West, with a six-goal rating. Among his acquaintances in sports was Tex Rickard, a famous boxing promoter and entrepeneur who was then based in New York.

The year before, Rickard had been looking for sporting events to stage in New York's vast Madison Square Garden, which was idle too much of the time to make economic sense. Rickard decided to put a professional hockey team into the Garden and thought rivalry with a team in Chicago would be added insurance for success. He contacted Major McLaughlin and found a willing friend. The major was as sporting with his money as with his polo stick. He liked the idea and formed a syndicate of more than one hundred of his society friends to secure and establish a National Hockey League franchise in Chicago.

The major already had noted the surging popularity of professional hockey in Canada, where the National Hockey League had been founded and had begun to prosper after World War I. So well had the league done that it even invaded the United States in 1924, placing a franchise in Boston, and in 1925, adding teams in New York and Pittsburgh.

In early 1926, the league was ready to add three more American franchises. Men with money were eager to make the plunge in Detroit and New York, which wanted a second team, and the first to step forward with his checkbook open in Chicago was Major McLaughlin. For $12,000 he and his associates were awarded a membership card in the NHL on May 15, 1926, and the right to call the team whatever nickname they wanted to. Major McLaughlin chose the name Black Hawks. During World War I the major had served as commander of the 333rd Machine-Gun Battalion of the 85th (Black Hawk) Division of the U.S. Army.

The division's nickname commemorated Black Hawk, the famous Indian chief of the early 1800's, who once had the honor of being pursued by young Abraham Lincoln. Chief Black Hawk also had been famed as an orator. His namesakes later became famed for making as much noise as any team in hockey.

The major, who sported a banker's mustache, also had the honor of being married to an extraordinary woman. He was the third husband of the famous dancer Irene Castle, who embarked on a screen career and a succession of mates after inventing the Castle Walk with her brother, Vernon. Mrs. McLaughlin contributed her talents to her husband's latest folly. She designed the uniforms, including the famous Indian head and the shoulder patches with the crossed hockey sticks.

By mid-summer of 1926 the Black Hawks were well on the way to being established. The only thing they lacked was players. On September 25, just two months before the season was to start, they got those—at one blow. Major McLaughlin was able to conclude a bargain transaction. The Western Canadian Hockey League was going broke and was auctioning off its players. The major bought the entire Portland (Oregon) team for $200,000. These Rosebuds, as the Portland team was nicknamed, were the Black Hawks who made their debut at the Coliseum. Actually, McLaughlin got his money's worth. The Rosebuds included some fine players. He picked up a few others in separate deals.

Among the original Black Hawks were such great players as Dick Irvin, Babe Dye, Mickey Macke, George Hay, Rabbit McVeigh, Percy Traub, and Hugh Lehman, a goaltender in his 19th season. Irvin later was to become famous as coach of the Montreal Canadiens and even—for a couple of terms—as coach of the Hawks. The veteran Dye had been the league's leading scorer the season before and was to top the Hawks in goals scored with 25 in 44 games their first year.

So it was quite a respectable team that took the ice on opening night, November 17, 1926, and defeated Toronto 4-1 to begin the long history of the Hawks.

3

Muldoon's Curse

MAJOR MCLAUGHLIN made only one serious mistake when he founded the Hawks in 1926. He hired a veteran hockey man, Pete Muldoon, to coach the team.

Since in their first year the Hawks finished a respectable third in the American Division of what then was the 10-team, two-division NHL, on the face of it the mistake doesn't seem obvious.

But that's only if you aren't aware of The Curse of the Muldoon, one of the hardiest and most colorful legends in hockey. And, despite wishful thinking and easy rationalization, The Curse has lost little of its potency over almost half a century.

It's a fact that the Hawks' history has been richer in star players than in championships. The Hawks won the Stanley Cup, the highest honor in hockey, only three times in their first 44 seasons. And only twice were they able to finish first in their division (actually, the only division in the NHL for 25 years).

Theirs has been a long tale of frustration despite occasional partial triumphs—and this although they have always had their share of great stars, as in Bobby Hull and Stan Mikita during the 1960's. Before that, players such as Johnny Gottselig, Charlie Gardiner, Mush March, Max and Doug Bentley, Bill Mosienko and Babe Dye were among the finest of their day. Yet seldom could these stars combine their talents to bring the Hawks to the top in Stanley Cup play. And for 41 years, until 1966-67, first place completely eluded them. As for putting the two together for a complete, satisfying triumph—the Stanley Cup and first place in the same season—that was entirely beyond the Hawks in their first 44 years.

There seems to be no rational explanation for such an extended history of frustration, especially as the Hawks so often would lead their division going into the final week or two of the season and then mysteriously would slide into second or third place.

But there is an irrational explanation and that's The Curse of the Muldoon. According to legend, Major Mc-Laughlin, an impulsive and dictatorial aristocrat, couldn't believe the players for whom he had paid $200,000 were anything less than first-place material. He told Muldoon so after the 1926-27 season and fired him. Muldoon, bitter at his dismissal, supposedly raised his hands solemnly and proclaimed in dire tones: "This team will never finish in first place." Then he stalked out of the astonished major's office, leaving behind him what became known as The Curse of the Muldoon. And as the Hawks built up an unblemished record of failure for more than four decades, the legend grew in majesty. It was solemnly revived every season by newspaper columnists and whispered about half uneasily in the Hawk locker room.

The legend, however, is a hoax, perpetrated by a Toronto newspaper columnist, James X. Coleman of the *Toronto Globe and Mail*, about 15 years after the supposed incident in McLaughlin's office. Hard put to find a subject for a column one day, Coleman became inventive and let his fancy roam. Inspired by the faintly recalled name of Muldoon, he wrote:

"The Hawks are victims of a hex Pete Muldoon put on them many years ago, after he was fired as coach. He had a stormy session with Major Frederic McLaughlin, the strange eccentric who owned the Hawks when they were admitted to the NHL in 1926.

"Muldoon coached the Hawks to a third-place finish in their first year, but McLaughlin was not impressed. 'This team was good enough to be first,' he said.

"Muldoon was amazed at McLaughlin's criticism, but not to the point of shutting up. 'You're crazy!' he fumed.

"McLaughlin was outraged by such heresy. 'You're fired!' he roared.

"Muldoon flared back in a black Irish snit. 'Fire ma, Major, and you'll never finish first! I'll put a curse on this team that will hoodoo it till the end of time!'

"And so, kiddies, that's why the Hawks always fail to grab the flag in the NHL. They cannot beat the Curse of the Muldoon . . ."

It was all a joke, of course, but the fact is that McLaughlin died in 1946 without ever seeing the Hawks finish first. And even through 1970 the Hawks hadn't yet truly finished first if one wants to consider that as winning both a divisional title and the Stanley Cup.

Nevertheless, win or lose, the Hawks almost always have been an exciting team, and for a time in the 1960's they had the greatest collection of stars in the game.

But by then it was a different game from what it was in the early days, when Muldoon supposedly invoked his curse. The fans of today, who thrill over the speed and power of Bobby Hull, the finesse and skill of Mikita, or the combination of both in Boston's Bobby Orr, probably would find the game less exciting if by some miracle they could be transported back in time to the early days. Today the ability to pass the puck forward from one zone to the next, from a player behind to a player ahead, is what lends so much speed and excitement to the game. This flashing of the puck forward and the style of play based on it—called "head-manning" the puck—has opened up hockey immensely.

Such play was impossible in 1926. At that time there

was no center red line. The ice was divided into only three zones with blue lines. Forward passing was permited only in the middle zone. The following season forward passes were permitted also in the defensive zone, and another year later forward passes could be made in all three zones. But even then all passes had to begin and be completed within a single zone. As a result, hockey was a slower game in those days and a premium was placed on stick-handling and the ability to move the puck up ice without passing. Gottselig, a Hawk as player, coach, and club official for 30 years, was the finest stick-handler of his day.

The major change in the game came in 1943-44 when the red line was put in at center ice. This meant that a pass could be started and completed anywhere in a team's half of the ice. A defenseman thus could whip the puck from even behind the goal line to a forward poised near the red line. This set up the fast break, the explosive play best demonstrated by such outstanding players as Bobby Hull and Montreal's Maurice (Rocket) Richard. As a result, far more goals are scored today than were scored in games 30 and 40 years ago. In those days 1-0 and 2-1 scores were common. They were almost the rule rather than the exception.

Whether hockey was better in the old days than it is now is beside the point. But the game was different. It wasn't just that the old-timers didn't score as many goals as today's players do. More to the point, they scored them differently.

Without doubt, however, the old-time players got hockey off to a great start on its way to becoming the major sport it is today.

4

Paddy's Legacy

HIS MONUMENT cost $6,000,000, but all that he had in the world when he left it was the $2.50 found in his pocket after he died. At that, it was more than Patrick T. (Paddy) Harmon's parents spent on his education, because he got it cheaply—on the streets of 19th century Chicago. The "monument" is the Chicago Stadium, that mammoth hall where hockey has climbed from a minor sports attraction to a major business enterprise whose gross income at the gate surpasses that of any other game in town.

The Black Hawks and the NHL owe much to the memory of Paddy Harmon, even though he never owned a major league franchise. He was a sports promoter with a vision, a "bullheaded Irishman," as his enemies called him, who wanted to build and did build the best sports arena in the world. In its day the Stadium perhaps was both.

He built it with $2,500,000 of his own money and the rest from friends—the "friends" who forced him out less than a year after the Stadium first opened, on March 28, 1929, and left him penniless when he died under his overturned car on July 22, 1930. But you couldn't beat Paddy's wake for style. It was held in the Stadium.

Paddy had a rule of thumb as a promoter. "It is not hard to please the public," he said. "All you have to do is remember that we are all born children, that we all die children, and that in between times we are children."

Harmon's link with hockey was slender, even though he provided the hall that eventually assured the sport's success in Chicago. He built his fortune on such varied promotions as dance halls, roller skating, boxing, and six-day bicycle racing.

Still, Paddy was one of the first men to attempt to bring to Chicago the game of hockey, which had boomed after World War I in Canada. If his attempt failed, it did so magnificently. Paddy showed up at an NHL expansion meeting in Montreal in 1926 carrying a black satchel. With great showmanship, he opened the satchel and carefully counted out a stack of fifty $1,000 bills on the conference table in front of the assembled NHL club owners. "There, gentlemen, is my bid of $50,000," he said. "Give me a franchise for Chicago and all this money is yours—and now."

The NHL owners, who shared all franchise money, merely looked sadly at Paddy's stack of $1,000 bills. It hurt, but dejectedly they had to turn him down. They already had sold the Chicago franchise, secretly, to Major McLaughlin for a mere $12,000.

Illustrative of the great growth of hockey since then is that in contrast with the $12,000 Major McLaughlin paid for the franchise in 1926 the owners of the six new franchises that joined the NHL in 1967 had to pay $2,000,000 apiece for the privilege and the two more admitted in 1970 had to put up $6,000,000.

Even if Paddy's bid for the Chicago franchise failed, it was his enterprise that ensured the survival of the Black Hawks and their eventual financial success. For it was he who put up the Stadium, which for more than 40 years was the largest indoor arena used for hockey in the country. Only New York's newest Madison Square Garden, opened in 1968, which seats 17,500, has a larger seating capacity for hockey than the Stadium, which seats a couple of hundred less. But since there is more room for standees in the Stadium, Chicago crowds are generally larger than those in New York. What's more, plans exist for enlarging the Stadium to a seating capacity of 27,000, which would make it again the largest arena in the NHL. Season after season it is standing-room-only for every Black Hawk game, with crowds averaging about 18,500 a game. Ironically, Paddy was already out of the Stadium picture by the time the Hawks got to play their first game there, December 16, 1929.

From the start Major McLaughlin had been aware that the ancient, small Coliseum was unsuited in the long run. It had been an adventure for high society the first time out, but the attraction began to pale. In later years the society that turned out was a different sort, to judge by the rotten eggs, dead fish, and even cherry bombs that were flung on the ice. But whatever class of people came to hockey games, they had to pay to get in and the Coliseum limited the amounts of money that could be taken in for top attractions. A move had to be made. There were nights when almost nobody, high or low society, came to see the Hawks in the Coliseum. The team almost went bankrupt, but it found new life by moving into the Stadium, whose management eventually was to assume control of the club.

The good times ahead were presaged by the 14,000 fans who turned out for that first game on Stadium ice December 16, 1929, and saw the Hawks whip Pittsburgh 3-1. In the Hawk lineup that night were a couple of youngsters, Harold (Mush) March and Johnny Gottselig, who later played important roles in the first two Stanley Cup championships, of 1933-34 and 1937-38.

From the beginning life in the Stadium was just as much fun as games, especially under Major McLaughlin, who ran the team for almost 20 years without knowing too much about hockey. He was aided in his erratic course chiefly by two men, both of whom enlisted at the start.

They were Bill Tobin, a squat man who became known as The Mysterious Mr. T, and Joseph Chesterfield Farrell, the publicity man whose resemblance to Abe Lincoln was only one of his notable characteristics.

Farrell already had a colorful career behind him when he came to the Hawks. As a young man, he had been a roommate of Theodore Dreiser in college, had sung with John Philip Sousa's band, had climbed the Pyramids and had been a song plugger before practising law and then turning to publicity. For the next thirty years he was to "sell" the Hawks and he did it with a rare enthusiasm. It was charged that in the early years he gave tickets away to all comers to induce them to attend the games, though years later he denied it:

"I didn't do that. What I did was this. I got the Major to give me introductions to the heads of some big companies. Then I'd go to their luncheons, say at Sears Roebuck, and have the head of the company go with me. I'd tell them the businessmen had brought this game to Chicago and wanted them to see it. If they just saw it they'd like it. And the heads of their companies wanted them to see the game once, as their guests. I'd tell them, 'If you want to go and take your family and friends, line up here for tickets. But don't take them if you don't want to go.'

"I guess some games I gave away 3,000 tickets, but I was right. It caught on, and the Hawks made money for the next 13 or 14 years, some years an unbelievable amount of money."

While Farrell pushed tickets, Tobin, a younger man in his early thirties, was the Major's man for all jobs. He was a Canadian who had wandered to Chicago, arriving according to some reports in 1926 with nothing more than a cardboard suitcase and enough money to buy a newspaper. Leafing through the paper he had noted that a hockey team was being formed in Chicago. Having had some experience in hockey, he decided to offer his services to Major McLaughlin. The major, being impressed with

Tobin, offered him $50 a week to become his secretary. Before long Tobin became general manager of the team and much later McLaughlin's successor as president and chief owner. In a pinch, he even coached the team.

Perhaps Tobin's greatest talent was the ability to survive the Major's whims and dictatorial ways. Once, when the Major demoted him to publicity director and made Farrell general manager, the change lasted only one week. One of the manager's major duties was to show up at 8:00 a.m. each morning in the Major's offices and listen to a two- or three-hour harangue from McLaughlin. Tobin had been able to show up and listen to perfection. Farrell didn't mind listening to the Major but hated to show up as early as 8:00 a.m. The Major graciously let them switch back to their old jobs.

Farrell was the more colorful of the pair, but Tobin wasn't without a sense of humor—as might be expected of a man who saw 20 coaches fired out from under him in the 20 years of the Major's rule.

One morning when Farrell was sitting at his desk Tobin stopped by on the way to his own office. After exchanging pleasantries Tobin asked, "You been back in the men's room this morning?" When Farrell said no, Tobin asked, "Are you sure?" Whereupon Farrell vehemently affirmed he should know whether he had been there or not.

"Okay," said Tobin. "I just found a dollar bill on the floor and thought it might be yours," then went on to his own office.

Farrell counted his money three times and finally said to his secretary, "You know, I think I did lose a buck somewhere . . ." But he didn't dare reopen the matter.

Farrell too was pretty tricky. Part of his job as publicity director was to entertain the press, which in those days meant providing bootleg liquor at inflated prices.

The Major never was known as a strict teetotaler but regarded rather as a sipper than a drinker. He frowned on expense accounts that included alcoholic refreshment for reporters on the hockey beat. Farrell had to find a cover-up for this; so he began listing the purchase of hockey pucks by the gross. One day the Major noticed the Hawks had a supply of pucks totaling half a dozen gross, which seemed somewhat excessive. He called in Farrell.

"What on earth are we doing with all these pucks?" he asked Farrell. "You've been ordering enough for the entire league, let alone for one team."

The nimble-witted Farrell replied, "Major, these pucks are worth their weight in gold in publicity. The hockey writers have been asking for them as souvenirs for their families and friends. This ought to help hockey no end."

To Farrell's surprise, the Major beamed all over the place. "That's just fine! Wonderful! Such interest is tremendous. Nothing can beat word-of-mouth publicity."

They were a wonderful trio, Major McLaughlin, Tobin, and Farrell. And under them the Hawks grew up fitfully, sometimes almost killed with the growing pains. There were more downs than ups, but with it all they survived.

5

The Age of Coaches

IN LATER years Johnny Gottselig had a stock answer for anyone who asked him, "Who was the worst coach you ever had in Chicago?"

"I don't know," Gottselig would say. "I'd say it was a photo finish between half a dozen of them."

Major McLaughlin was a man of uncertain temper but with a sure trigger finger as evidenced by the fact that in the first 10 years of his regime he hired and fired 13 coaches. Occasionally a man would last a campaign or two, but to even it out the Major would run through two or three the following season.

Muldoon's successor for the 1927-28 season was Barney Stanley, who went just halfway into the campaign before he was replaced by ex-goaltender Lehman. Between the two of them they guided the Hawks to seven victories, 34 defeats, and three ties. The next season, in which the Hawks again won just seven games, McLaughlin ran through three coaches, Herb Gardiner, Tom Shaughnessy, and Tobin, who had to be pressed into service. It was Dick Irvin's turn after that, and his dismissal on a morning in 1931, after the Hawks had lost a game the night before, was a perfect illustration of the Major's decisiveness. Disconsolate, Irvin strolled into the Major's office.

"For the life of me, Major, I don't know what's wrong with this team," Irvin lamented.

"I'll tell you what's wrong," snapped McLaughlin. "All you have to do is look in that big mirror over there."

That was the end of Irvin as Hawk coach until a brief return near the end of his life in the mid-1950's. In between, he built up a great succession of winners at Montreal. Firing him was one of the Major's greatest mistakes. But he erred more often in whom he hired.

One of McLaughlin's most notable selections was Godfrey Matheson, whom he hired in 1932 after a chance meeting on a railroad train. In an age of colorful characters, Matheson was a standout.

Len Bramson, a sportswriter, described Matheson this way:

"He was a studious, almost ascetic-looking man. He herded the Hawks to Pittsburgh for training and on the first day turned up with shin pads over his trousers, elbow pads around his knees, a tassel cap on his head and two buckets of pucks.

"The first practice was unique. Matheson kept flipping pucks on the ice and the players skated by and shot them at the net. But he wouldn't let Charlie Gardiner go in goal for fear he would get hurt by one of the flying pucks.

"After a few hours, Matheson picked a team of six players and while the others sat on the bench he told them, 'Now this will be my first team. I want you to watch them, paying particular regard to each individual, so that you can adapt yourself to his style. Then, if you have to go into a game, you'll be able to fit in.'

"For the next five days, the first team skated up and down and tauntingly yelled, 'Don't you guys wish you could make the first team?' All the while the reserves sat along the boards, loafing, smoking and doing nothing to keep in shape.

Matheson's tactics during games also were unusual. He got the notion that the way to score goals was to have Taffy Abel, a 230-pound defenseman, follow on the heels of quick-skating Mush March, the tiny 5-foot 5 inch forward who was a fine stick-handler and shooter. The idea was for March to carry the puck into the opposing defense-men, splitting them, then leaving the puck for Abel to carry into the net with brute force. It didn't quite work out, and Matheson was replaced as coach by Emil Iverson, who was replaced by Tommy Gorman just a few weeks later.

Under this kind of transient coaching and whimsical ownership great players came and went as the Hawks and the NHL grew up together. Among the finest Hawks of the 1930's were Gottselig, March, goalie Gardiner, center Howie Morenz and defenseman Earl Seibert. Morenz probably was the greatest player to wear a Hawk uniform before the days of Bobby Hull and Stan Mikita, although he did not arrive in Chicago until near the end of a long and brilliant career. In 1923, Morenz, then 21, joined the Montreal Canadiens and 11 years later was traded by them to the Hawks for the 1934-35 season. John P. Carmichael, later sports editor of the *Chicago Daily News,* at that time was the newspaper's hockey writer. Carmichael got to know Morenz well on the long, tiring train trips to which the athletes of those days were doomed.

Morenz told Carmichael the tale of his "baptism" as a full-fledged member of the Canadiens. There can be no better account of what hockey and the men in it were like in the early days.

Here is Carmichael's account:

"The doctor took six stitches in Bernie Morris's scalp and then walked out of the Calgary dressing room. He made his way through lines of excited fans jabbering over the last period's play to the quarters of the Canadiens and paused in front of a young man.

" 'What did you hit him for?' the doctor asked. 'I just took six stitches in his head. . . . What did he do?'

" 'Nothing, I guess,' growled the player, twisting steel-shod feet on the wooden floor. 'I just lost my head. I didn't mean it.'

" 'Well, I'd keep my glimmers open if I was you,' the

doctor remarked. 'Dutton and Gardiner have vowed that you'll never walk off the ice tonight.'

"The kid, Howie Morenz, nodded appreciatively and filed out of the door, one of a long scarlet line that clumped awkwardly up the runway and out onto the ice into the midst of a shrieking, packed arena. Mechanically, he glanced at Red Dutton and Herb Gardiner, the two Calgary defensemen.

"Play began where it left off. . . . In a trice, Morenz, the kid, playing in his first 'World Series' forgot everything but the game. No wonder then, as he gathered in the disc behind his own net and started to streak down center ice, he had forgotten all about Dutton and Gardiner.

"But they hadn't forgotten. Coming toward them they saw not only a possible goal but the fresh kid who had cut open one of their men. As a unit, they moved toward him.

"The three of them met at the Calgary blue line with a crack that was still echoing from the rafters as the referee's whistle stopped play and the Canadiens rushed to the spot where Morenz, unconscious, lay in a bloody-red heap. They carried him off the ice a few minutes later, his left collar bone broken. In the clubroom, the same doctor who had warned him fingered through a preliminary examination. Morenz opened his eyes.

" 'Well, doc,' he said in a shaky voice, 'they kept their word, didn't they? I couldn't walk off.' "

Morenz didn't walk off the ice in the final game of his hockey career, either. Traded by the Hawks to New York in January 1936, he found his way back to the Canadiens by the next season. On January 28, 1937, in a game against the Hawks at the Montreal Forum, Morenz tried to swing around defenseman Earl Seibert, who threw a solid check into him. Morenz, a little man at 5 feet 7, went flying through the air, his skates striking the boards. A skate imbedded itself in the wood and Morenz suffered a broken leg. Seven weeks later, on March 8, 1937, Morenz died of a heart attack at the age of 35.

Morenz was the Bobby Hull of his day, the man who popularized hockey in the United States because of his flashy skating style and his uncanny perception of what an opposing goalie would do. He scored an average of a goal every two games and was the most highly paid player in hockey, getting $15,000 a season during the great depression. At that time the average player was doing well to earn $3,000, and teams were bound by agreement to pay all their players a total of not more than $65,000.

Major McLaughlin had been glad enough to pay Morenz a "high" salary, hoping that Howie would prove a solid enough attraction to turn in a profit at the gate. But generally the Major was as tough on his players as on his coaches. After all, tickets sold at a $2 top in those days and were hard to sell. Charlie Gardiner, the Hawks' great goaltender and now in the Hall of Fame, never earned more than $5,000 a season. In fact, the season after Gardiner won a Vezina Trophy as the league's top goalie, the Major tried to cut his pay by $500. Fortunately for Gardiner, the story got into the newspapers and the Major, grumbling at the "meddlesome press," restored the $500.

Yet one shouldn't be too hard on the old Major. Either he or Irvin, before the latter's abrupt dismissal, had come up with a new hockey concept, the use of three forward lines. The Major, always a military man, seized at the idea. Outnumber and wear down the opposition! Hockey players should thank him, because it opened up a lot of jobs. And, put to good use by Coach Gorman in the 1933-34 season, it brought the Hawks their first Stanley Cup.

The Hawks didn't have the best players that year, but they had depth, a quality that seemed to escape them in future seasons.

6

The Silver Age Begins

UNTIL the spring of 1934 the Hawk's record in Stanley Cup play was a tale of unrelieved frustration. Only in 1930-31 did they reach the finals, then to be cut down by the Canadiens in Montreal 2-0 in the fifth and deciding game.

But Major McLaughlin and Coach Tom Gorman had good reason for optimism when the 1934 play-offs opened. Gorman, a jovial, bluff Irishman, had been given a chance to get acquainted with his players. The unpredictable Major had left him in charge for a season and a half. At this time the Hawks were well worth getting acquainted with. The reliance on old hand-me-down players was over. Such young stars as Gottselig, March, Paul Thompson, Taffy Abel, Lionel Conacher and goalie Gardiner combined into a formidable team.

The best of course was Gardiner, who took over as goalie from Lehman in the 1928-29 season. He was an aggressive Scotsman born in Edinburgh and raised in Winnipeg. Many old-timers consider him the finest goalie ever. Gardiner's goals-against average for seven seasons was 2.13, and he had 42 shutouts in 316 games. In 21 play-off games he had five shutouts and a 1.67 goals-against average. He won the Vezina Trophy twice and was selected to the All-Star team four times. Francis

(King) Clancy, in later years assistant coach of the Toronto Maple Leafs and an outstanding defenseman during
his playing peak in the 1920s, unhesitatingly chose Gardiner as the finest goalie of all time. "Charlie had everything," said Clancy, "sure hands, good eyes, quick reflexes, no weak spots, and a fine team spirit. In his last
season of 48 games, 10 of them were shutouts and in 14
others he allowed only one goal.

"He also had a lot of fun in him. I remember the night
someone threw a derby hat on the ice. Charlie skated over,
picked up the lid, slipped it on his head as though it was a
helmet and wore it while playing."

A remarkable—and ominous—aspect of Gardiner's
spectacular play during the 1933-34 season was that he
was intermittently ill yet never missed a game.

The key offensive unit for the Hawks was the line cen-
tered by Elwyn (Doc) Romnes, which had March at right
wing and Paul Thompson at left wing. Thompson led in
scoring with 20 goals. Lou Trudel centered the line with
Gottselig at left wing and Don McFadyen at right wing.
Gottselig scored 19 goals. Other forwards were Tommy
Cook, Rosario (Lolo) Couture, Leroy Goldsworthy, John
Sheppard, Bill Kendall and Jack Leswick.

Thanks to the generosity of the Montreal Canadiens, the
Hawks went into the season with a much strengthened
defense. The Canadiens shipped Lionel Conacher to the
Hawks, apparently as punishment for disregarding training
rules. Conacher, superb in every sport and later chosen
Canada's Athlete of the Half-Century (1901-1950),
teamed up with Taffy Abel on one back line. Not only
was Conacher outstanding as a "policeman" but he contributed 10 goals to the offense. Art Coulter and Roger
Jenkins were the other defensive pair. It was an outstanding team with outstanding players, who left enduring names
in the game.

Gottselig, born in Odessa, Russia, in 1905, was tall and
slender. He was a superb stick-handler and led the Hawks

in scoring three times during his first five seasons with them. He played 15 years.

Thompson, a veteran acquired from the New York Rangers, during eight seasons with the Hawks led them in scoring six times. He was chosen to the All-Star team twice. In 1939 he became coach of the Hawks and lasted five full seasons, being replaced in 1945 by Gottselig for a three-year term.

The fans' favorite, however, was little March, who played 17 seasons with the Hawks. Like many small men, he compensated for lack of size with extra fire and was considered one of the outstanding right wings of the day.

At the conclusion of the regular season, the Major was a little less grumpy than usual. The Hawks finished with a winning record, ending up second to the Detroit Red Wings in the American Division. They won 20 games, lost 17 and tied 11. They didn't exactly roll over the Canadiens in the first round of the play-offs, but defeated them 3-2 in the first game and tied the second 1-1 to take the series four goals to three (in those days the preliminary play-offs were decided on total goals for two games).

It was March who scored the final goal of the series for the Hawks, a portent of what was to come. Gottselig got a pair of goals in the first game and Conacher the other.

Gardiner made the second round a little easier. He shut out the Montreal Maroons 3-0 and the Hawks also won the second game, 3-2 to take the series 6 goals to 2.

Now came the greatest hurdle, the division champion Red Wings in the finals for the Stanley Cup. It took courage to bet on the Hawks with the best-of-five games series starting with the first two contests in Detroit, where Chicago hadn't won a game in more than four years. Unbelievably, the Hawks took the first two games at Detroit. They won the opener 2-1 in overtime with Thompson scoring the decisive goal after more than 20 minutes of extra play. The second victory came easier, the Hawks rolling over Detroit 4-1.

Not to be outdone in bucking the odds against the visiting team, Detroit turned around to win the third game 5-2 at the Stadium, keeping the series alive. Wilf Cude, Detroit goalie, turned in a remarkable performance, considering that Hawk Couture broke his nose midway in the second period with an accidental whack of the stick.

While Cude suffered only physical damage, Gardiner suffered in spirit and mind. He was shattered by the defeat and came near to a nervous breakdown. It was considered unlikely he would be able to play goal for the Hawks in the fourth game, scheduled for two days later.

"The management sent him to Milwaukee for two days of rest," said Gottselig. "We really didn't think he would be able to play. He was always alone, the nervous type. He worried a lot and losing a game always seemed to take a lot out of him."

Gardiner returned from his brief holiday, however, for the fourth game. And the Hawks still had the edge in the series, leading two games to one, with this game to be played on their ice. A crowd of almost 18,000 turned out to cheer them on to a Stanley Cup the night of April 10, 1934. It was a long night of cheering and frustration. Excitement built up during three regulation periods of play without a goal. And when the first overtime period had been completed the scoreboard still showed Black Hawks 0, Red Wings 0.

The game went deep into the second overtime period. The Hawks, obviously the superior team this night, were dominating play, rushing twice to every Red Wing drive, and controlling the puck most of the time. The break came when Ebbie Goodfellow, Red Wing defenseman, was sent to the penalty box. Now the Hawks had a one-man advantage and pressed to make the best of it. But the Red Wing penalty killers broke up the first Hawk rush. And when Romnes, Thompson, and March started on another sweep down ice a whistle from the referee halted play.

The face-off was in Red Wing territory. Romnes took the face-off and with a single motion whipped the puck back to little March.

"I was standing behind the face-off circle," said March. "The puck came right to me, about 40 feet out from Wilf Cude. All I had to do was to take a couple of steps and fire. I put everything I had on that one."

Cude already had stopped 52 shots on goal, and for a moment, while the crowd of 18,000 screamed, it looked as if he were going to stop this one. But the explosive power of March's well-muscled arms was too much for the goalie, who kicked out his right leg, caught a piece of the puck about two feet off the ice, but then saw it spin into the webbing behind him.

The red light signaling the goal flashed on, and the Stadium erupted with a tremendous roar. After 30 minutes and five seconds of overtime play the Black Hawks won their first Stanley Cup. Strangely, March, the man who had scored the biggest goal in Hawk history up to that time, wasn't just sure how the puck went in.

"I don't know whether Cude missed it or not," said March. "I always thought it went through his legs."

It really didn't matter to March at the moment. Without hesitation, he jumped into the net after the puck to get a souvenir with a meaning for a lifetime.

"I think Cude was startled to see me diving in after it," laughed March many years later, "but I just had to have it. It was probably the biggest goal I ever scored."

Certainly he scored few as important as this, although he had many good nights in hockey during a 17-year career. And nothing could ever match that moment. The smallest man in the league had become a giant, the hero of Chicago. Lou Trudell and other teammates hoisted March to their shoulders and paraded him around the rink while the fans gave him an ovation.

Even more deserving of acclaim was goalie Gardiner, who had turned aside 40 Detroit shots on goal through

90 minutes and five seconds of Stanley Cup play. In the eight games of the play-offs he lost just one game, tied another, and recorded two shutouts. No one could quarrel with Coach Gorman's praise: "He's the greatest goalie that ever donned the pads. He won the title for the Black Hawks. Without him, we wouldn't have made it."

Teammate Roger Jenkins had to pay off a bet to Gardiner—a bet that he couldn't stop the Red Wings. In payment, Jenkins wheeled Gardiner through the streets of the Chicago Loop in a wheelbarrow.

But Gardiner's moment of triumph was brief. Eight weeks later, on June 13, 1934, the goaltender supreme was dead. He had collapsed on a Winnipeg street and died shortly after of a brain tumor, perhaps the result of being struck in the head by a puck earlier in his career.

Coach Gorman's time of triumph with the Hawks didn't last much longer. He had guided the team to the Stanley Cup but that apparently wasn't enough for Major McLaughlin. Shortly after the season ended, Gorman joined the Major's list of coaches who wouldn't be missed.

Although Gorman went on to further triumphs elsewhere, he achieved another distinction during his brief term with the Hawks in addition to the first Stanley Cup. He was the only coach who ever lost a game for them by forfeit. It happened on March 14, 1933, at Boston. The Hawks were leading 2-1 with just two seconds left in the game when Boston's Eddie Shore, the great defenseman, tied the score. At that time, even during the regular season, games tied at the end of the regulation 60 minutes went into overtime. A 10-minute period was allotted to settle the issue, and if the tie wasn't broken during that time, the game was declared a draw.

Boston didn't waste any time getting started in the overtime period, Marty Barry scoring shortly after the teams resumed play; but the goal was disputed by the Hawks. Referee Bill Stewart (who also had a long career as a National League umpire in baseball) skated over to the

Hawks' bench the better to hear Gorman's complaints. Suddenly, Gorman pulled Stewart's sweater over his head and began battering the blinded referee with his fists. Stewart, finally pulling down his sweater, landed a couple of punches himself on Gorman.

"You're out of the game," Stewart roared. "Leave the rink or it'll cost you that much more."

"If I go, my players go," roared back Gorman, standing his ground. Stewart called the police to eject Gorman, whereupon the players followed their coach into the dressing room.

"I'll give you one minute to get back on the ice," Gorman yelled after the retreating Hawks. The minute passed and the Hawks failed to reappear.

Stewart motioned to the Boston team to take up positions for a face-off. He dropped the puck at mid-ice and Boston's Cooney Weiland picked up the disc, skated toward the empty Hawk net and scored. The final score was recorded as 1-0 in favor of Boston for the only forfeit game in NHL history.

Ironically, it was Stewart, the referee who had humiliated them, who coached the Hawks to their second Stanley Cup.

7

A "Shot" and a Goalie

MAJOR MCLAUGHLIN had a dream, a red-white-and-blue dream, and it distressed him that almost all his players had to be imported from Canada.

"Someday, we'll be able to put a team of Americans on the ice," he'd say. "Think of what that will mean to attendance. American cities will be represented by American players."

Then he would sigh and go back to dealing for more Canadian players, who still were incontestably the best.

One of the biggest trading sprees came after winning the Stanley Cup in 1934. With Gardiner dead, the Hawks needed a goalie, and Taffy Abel had retired to open a hole among the defensemen. Fortunately, when the Major had fired Coach Gorman, the resilient Irishman had landed on his feet as manager of the Montreal Canadiens. He was able to act as a go-between in a series of deals between the Hawks and Canadiens. Somehow the Hawks lost Lionel Conacher, the All-Star defenseman, to Montreal in these transactions and wound up with aging Howie Morenz and a veteran goalie, Loren Chabot, who was 35 and sinking.

Luckily, the Hawks also made a deal with Toronto. They obtained defenseman Alex Levinsky and found a separate prize in another backliner, Art Wiebe, who was to become an All-Star and play 10 seasons with Chicago. The Major didn't know what to expect of his rebuilt team and certainly didn't expect much of his new coach, Clem Loughlin, a former Hawk defenseman. Both surprised him in the 1934-35 season, particularly because aging goalie Chabot surprised the league by being just about as good as Gardiner had been. He had eight shutouts in 48 games and his 1.83 goals-against average earned him the Vezina Trophy and a place on the All-Star team. As a result, the Hawks had their finest regular season record in the first three decades of their history. They won 26 games, lost 17, and tied five to finish second in the American Division. Even bowing out of the play-offs in the first round couldn't take the edge off that.

McLaughlin was so shocked that he left Loughlin in charge for two more seasons, to give him a record three-year run among Hawk coaches. But it wasn't accomplished without suffering on Loughlin's part.

In the first place, the Hawks began to descend the next year, winning just 21 games and having to be satisfied with third place. The next season, 1936-37, was even worse, as they won just 14 games and missed the play-offs altogether.

But what really hurt was that the Major was overcome by his red-white-and-blue dream, and forced Loughlin to carry it out before sending him to join the ghosts of his predecessors as Hawk coaches.

With just five games left in the 1936-37 season and the Hawks already out of play-off berth contention, the Major decided to experiment with a team of American-born players.

He had a solid core for such a team in four true big-leaguers. Goalie Mike Karakas, who had replaced Chabot, was born in Aurora, Minnesota. Levinsky was a native of Syracuse, New York. Doc Romnes came from White Bear, Minnesota. Trudell's birthplace was Salem, Massachusetts.

The Major added five more Yanks for his test. They

were all rookies: defensemen Ernest Klingbeil of Hancock, Michigan, and Butch Schaefer of Eveleth, Minnesota; wings Al Suomi of Eveleth and Bun Laprairie of Sault Ste. Marie, Michigan; and center Milt Brink of Eveleth.

On March 11, 1937, the Major unveiled his Yankee dandies against the Boston Bruins at the Stadium. Boston won 6-2, and none of the new players scored, but Klingbeil and Schaefer were both on defense for every Bruin goal.

Art Ross of the Bruins was enraged by the Major's experiment and demanded he be stripped of the Chicago franchise.

"It's the most farcical thing ever attempted," charged Ross. "It's a disgrace to hockey. The rookies didn't get a shot on goal."

Other officials in the league also protested that such experiments shouldn't be conducted when teams were still battling for play-off positions. McLaughlin told them to mind their own business. His Yanks almost made the Major look good for a brief time. The Toronto Maple Leafs were lucky in beating the Hawks 3-2 in the next game, and Klingbeil scored a goal and became the star. Then the youngsters dropped the New York Rangers 4-3 before sinking out of sight in the last two games of the experiment, 9-4 before the New York Americans and 6-1 at the hands of the angry Bruins.

With a sigh, the Major concluded the time was not yet ripe for staffing the Black Hawks entirely with American-born players. He also concluded that the time was ripe for sacking Coach Loughlin, who had worn out three average welcomes for Hawk coaches. In his place the Major appointed the irascible referee Bill Stewart, the man who had handed the Hawks the only forfeit defeat in hockey history four years before.

The benefits of Stewart's coaching weren't readily apparent when the Hawks ended the 1937-38 regular season. Sure, they had captured a play-off spot, but a 14-25-9 record didn't exactly make them a fierce contender for the

Stanley Cup. They went into the play-offs with a little less than hope and a little more than resignation. No matter what else happened, the season at least had been notable for the development of a fine center in Cully Dahlstrom, who won the Calder Trophy as rookie of the year. Few of the Hawk players had much hope. The attitude of Levinsky, in later years a furniture dealer in Toronto, perhaps was typical: "We were so bad that I thought we'd be eliminated in our first play-off series by the Canadiens. So I packed all my clothes in my car and sent my wife home to Toronto. But we kept winning and I was still living out of the car a month later."

Still, the Hawks had many of the players who had carried them to a Stanley Cup four years before. Gottselig and Thompson were still at their peaks, one or the other leading the team in scoring every season from 1929-30 through 1938-39. March and Rommes, two other heroes of the 1933-34 winners, were back for another shot. And if Lionel Conacher was gone, Earl Seibert, a veteran defenseman added in 1935, probably was his superior for steady play. Certainly, Mike Karakas was a steady goalie, although no one would venture to compare him with Gardiner.

It wasn't a brilliant team that the Hawks sent into the 1937-38 play-offs, but given the breaks it was one that had a chance of winning. The break it did get was one of the strangest in the history of the NHL—in the form of the goalie "nobody wanted," a journeyman named Alfie Moore. Moore, of course, has become a legend, and it's easy to forget that before he had a chance to work his "miracle" the Hawks had to do a little spadework on their own. They did that by beating the Montreal Canadiens twice after losing the opener of the three-game quarter-finals. A 4-0 shutout by Karakas and a goal by Thompson to break a 2-2 tie in the third game accomplished the reversal. And they did that by beating the New York Americans twice after losing the first game of the three-game semi-finals. A 1-0 shutout by Karakas and a winning goal by Romnes in the third game to provide the 3-2 margin accomplished the reversal.

The Hawks already had plenty of underdog in them before the stage was set for the Moore saga. And it's ironic that Moore's exploit should have so completely submerged the feats of superior players such as Karakas, Thompson, Romnes, Gottselig, and the rest. But it's a good story and even three decades later Gottselig remembered almost every detail of it.

It started when Karakas broke a toe in the last game against the Americans, leaving the Hawks temporarily without a goalie to start the final series against Toronto.

"We had sent Paul Goodman, our spare goalie, home before the play-offs started," recalled Gottselig. "There was no way of getting him to Toronto before the game that night (April 5, 1938). So that morning, at the usual club meeting, we were trying to determine whom we could use.

"At that time, Dave Kerr was goaltender of the New York Rangers and Coach Stewart was so hopeful that Conn Smythe (Toronto manager) would give us permission to use him. But Conn wouldn't go for that. He recommended Moore, a goalie he had kept at Pittsburgh (then a minor league team) all year."

Smythe's reluctance to let the Hawks use Kerr was understandable. Kerr had led the league in shutouts that season and had a 2.00 goals-against average. When Stewart, however, was informed of Smythe's veto of Kerr, he was so enraged he ran into a corridor and threatened to beat the daylights out of the Toronto manager. But after the usual pushing and shoving and verbal warfare, Stewart gave in. He agreed to try Moore.

"After seeing Smythe," continued Gottselig, "Stewart called a meeting at 1 o'clock that afternoon and told us what Conn had said. He asked if we knew anything about Moore. Since I said I knew him, he sent me and Paul Thompson to get him.

"We went to Moore's house, but his wife said he was at a corner tavern. We looked in there, but the bartender told us that Moore had left an hour before. He told us there was another tavern two or three blocks away.

"So we went there and, as luck would have it, Moore was sitting at the bar when we came in. He turned around and when he saw me his face lit up. 'Geez, I'm glad to see you. How about a couple of tickets to the game tonight?' he said.

"I'm glad to see you Alfie," I said. "You're going to get the best seat in the house."

"What are you talking about?" he asked, but we didn't have time to argue. We hustled him down to the hotel just the way he was. When Stewart saw him, he said, 'Get him out of here. I don't want him.' But we convinced Bill there wasn't anything else we could do. We got Alfie up to the rink, got him into uniform, put some coffee into him and sobered him up.

"While we were warming him up, Stewart said, 'Take it easy—don't shoot too hard. I don't want him hurt.' But Alfie was stopping everything, laughing and waving at his friends. He was mad at Smythe for sending him to Pittsburgh and said, 'I'll show him.'

"When the game started, Gordie Drillon of Toronto put the first shot past Alfie and we figured it would be like that the rest of the game. But they couldn't get anything else past him, and we got three goals to win the game.

"I got two of the goals and I figured I'd get a mention in the newspapers, but it was all Alfie Moore. He was all over the headlines. I was just mentioned in the summary.

"Toronto wouldn't let him play the next game. They got the president of the league to declare him ineligible. We'd gotten our spare goalie, Goodman, back and Smythe figured, 'To hell with you guys.' So we had to use Goodman and he hadn't skated in two weeks. They broke us up in that game, which also was at Toronto.

"But we had figured that if we could win just one game at Toronto we'd win the cup. And that's the way it worked out. We got 'em back to Chicago, where Karakas was ready, and won the two games there and the cup."

As Gottselig suggested, Toronto literally "broke up" the Hawks in the second game, winning 5-1 over Goodman, who reportedly was found 2½ hours before game time in a movie theatre. Toronto defenseman Red Horner cross-checked Doc Romnes and broke his nose in six places. March was knocked out of action. But three days later, on April 7, 1938, when the series moved to Chicago, the Hawks were ready. Karakas, fitted with a special boot to guard his toe, was back in goal. Romnes was outfitted with a football helmet with faceguard to protect his nose.

A crowd of 18,497, a new record for the NHL, watched in delight as the Hawks ganged up on Horner, and Romnes scored the decisive goal that gave them a 2-1 victory over Toronto. Romnes, who had won the Lady Byng Trophy for gentlemanly conduct two seasons before, led the assault on Horner to prove he could play it both ways.

Three days later, with Dahlstrom, Carl Voss, Jack Shill and March scoring goals, the Hawks won 4-1 to delight another huge Stadium turnout, capturing their second Stanley Cup in five years.

And, of course, the legend of Alfie Moore, "the goalie nobody wanted," was given eternal life. The Hawks were properly appreciative of his services. When the series ended, Bill Tobin asked Alfie what he thought his services were worth. Alfie guessed $150.

"That's not enough," said Tobin, and he peeled off three hundred dollar bills from his roll and thrust them into Alfie's hands. There was more to come. When the Hawks celebrated their Stanley Cup with a party Moore was invited and presented with a suitably engraved gold watch. In later years, Alfie's contribution was disparaged.

"There are some fanciful stories about Moore and Stewart," said Thompson later, "but we really won the cup by roughing up Horner. We cut him down gangland style." Maybe so, but there is no question Moore was in goal for the Hawks when they won the pivotal game and that he held Toronto to one goal. Drunk or not, he sobered Toronto.

"We threw everything at him but the house," insisted Turk Broda, the Toronto goalie in the series.

Moore was contented. He had had his moment, his spark of glory.

And so had the Hawks for almost a quarter of a century to come. Another 23 years were to pass before their next Stanley Cup. But that was unforeseeable then, and Major McLaughlin was basking in the glorious present, made even sweeter by an oddity of the team that had proved the best in hockey. Almost 50 per cent of the Hawk players were U.S. born: Mike Karakas, Alex Levinsky, Carl Voss, Roger Jenkins, Elwyn Romnes, Louis Trudel, Virgil Johnson, and Cully Dahlstrom. The Major's red-white-and-blue dream almost turned into a reality. He was so deliriously happy that he kept Coach Stewart, who had won a championship in his first season, until the following January before firing him.

8

Twenty-One Seconds to Glory

THE PUCK came from center Gus Bodnar, and Bill Mosienko barely got his stick on it before racing toward New York Ranger goalie Lorne Anderson. The goalie moved out of the net to cut down the angle on Mosienko, whom he knew only by reputation. Anderson was a rookie, nervous and unsure of himself. Mosienko was the fastest skater among the Black Hawks and one of the fastest in the league. As Anderson came out, Mosienko swerved into the slot, the area directly in front of the goal, faked a shot to the goalie's left, then snapped the puck with a flick of his wrist to the right into the net. That goal, at 6:09 of the third period on March 23, 1952, in the final game of the season at old Madison Square Garden in New York, was just a starter for Mosienko, then 29 years old.

On the following face-off, Bodnar again controlled the puck and got it over to Mosienko on right wing. Once more Mosienko sped down ice and once again he beat the helpless Anderson with a shot into the nets. This goal came at 6:20, just 11 seconds after the first one. After raising his stick in the traditional scoring salute for the second time, Mosienko again circled back to the center-ice face-off circle. Once more Bodnar beat his Ranger rival on the face-off, but this time whipped the puck over to left wing George Gee, who led this assault on Anderson. Anderson committed himself to guarding against Gee, but without hesitation the left wing passed the puck to Mosienko, coming in on the right. Mosienko pulled the trigger instantly and the puck shot by Anderson. The time was 6:30.

Mosienko had scored three goals within 21 seconds, setting a record that appears unbeatable. And, despite Anderson's inexperience in the NHL, the goals weren't flukes. A reporter wrote after the game: "Anderson might have stopped Mosienko's first shot, an open thrust from the center alley. But the second and third goals were neatly executed and could have fooled any goalie in the league." Although Mosienko's feat resulted in a 7-6 victory for the Hawks, even the partisan New York crowd of 3,254 "cheered Mosienko with a volume that seemed to come from twice the number of throats when the record-breaking accomplishment was announced."

Mosienko, a slightly built man of medium height, was one of the brightest Hawk stars of a dismal era, the twenty years that passed between the Stanley Cup championship of 1937-38 and the rebirth of the team in the late 1950's.

When the season that followed the Stanley Cup triumph opened, it would have been hard to believe that the Hawks were destined to wallow in the doldrums for two decades. The Major, proud of his champions, had spent lavishly to keep them on top. The Montreal Maroons had folded, and the Hawks bought the entire line of Baldy Northcott, Russ Blinco, and Earl Robinson. Louis Trudel was traded to the Canadiens for Joffre Desilets. During the season, Doc Romnes was swapped to Toronto for Bill Thoms.

The Hawks opened the 1938-39 season with the "greatest team ever," according to the experts. All Coach Stewart would have to do is push the buttons. It was the Major who pushed the button—on the ejector seat. The Hawks started out well enough, but then won just three of 17 games, and on January 2, 1939, Coach Stewart was fired. He was replaced by Paul Thompson, who was to last more than six seasons.

They were seasons of sorrow, as were those of his successors for two decades to come. Yet even those dreary years were made bearable for the fans by a succession of great players and occasional fine moments, comparable with Mosienko's feat of scoring three goals in 21 seconds.

Most spectacular among the many good players the Hawks had in the 1940's and early 1950's were the Bentley brothers, Max and Doug, who with Mosienko for a time formed hockey's most formidable scoring combination, "The Pony Line." And there was left wing Gee, who was almost as fast on his skates as Mosienko.

Gottselig, who succeeded Thompson as coach in April 1945 and kept the job for three years, had been one of the first hockey men to size up the talents of Mosienko and Gee. He got his first look at them when they were 17 while he was briefly managing the Kansas City minor league team.

"I formed a line with the two kids, playing center for them," he recalled. "I was a basket case after every game. I was 34 then, and it was murder trying to keep up with those two kids, especially Mosienko."

From the time Mosienko joined the Hawks during the 1941-42 season until the close of his career 13 years later, the NHL found it "murder" to keep up with him. Oddly, he scored two goals within 21 seconds in his first NHL game in 1942—and against the same Rangers whom he was to shock with his "instant hat trick" a decade later. During his career, Mosienko scored 258 goals, hitting a peak of 32 in 1943-44. Even 20 years later, only Bobby Hull and Stan Mikita had passed him up on the Hawk's all-time goal-scoring list.

(For comparisons between today's scorers and those of the past it must be noted that the number of games played by the NHL in a season has been increased several times. The league started with a 44-game schedule in 1926-27, went to 48 games in 1931-32, to 50 games in 1942-43, then to 60 games in 1946-47. Another increase to 70 games came in 1949-50, and that held until 1967-68 when 74 games were played. The next two seasons were of 76 games, then two more were added for 1970-71).

Mosienko was the natural replacement for March, the great veteran right wing who came to the end of his career in 1945. He was a clean player and in 1944-45 went the entire season without a penalty minute, winning the Lady Byng Trophy, as well as being selected an All-Star.

Mosienko was to find in the Bentley brothers, who also came along in the early 1940's, the perfect partners with whom to display his talent. Max at center, Doug at left wing, and Mosienko at right wing formed a line comparable with the Hawks' Scooter Line of Stan Mikita, Kenny Wharram, and Doug Mohns in the late 1960's.

It was Gottselig who as coach in 1946 put the Bentleys and Mosienko together to form the "Pony Line," and no one appreciated their talents more.

"He was one of the marvels of the game," Gottselig said of Doug Bentley, born in 1916 and four years older than Max. "He was the smallest of any of the great players, smaller than Howie Morenz. He was a crowd pleaser, always in the thick of things, driving down the middle. I would put him in the class of Morenz."

Doug was 5 feet, 8 inches and weighed 140 pounds. Max was 5 feet, 10 inches and weighed 155 pounds. Doug came to the Hawks in 1939-40 and Max a year later. A third Bentley, Reggie, got a brief trial with the Hawks in 1943 but failed to last. The two Bentleys were good enough for three ordinary players. Doug led the NHL in goals with 33 in 1942-43 and 38 in 1943-44 (in 50 games), also leading in total points the first year with 73. Max led the scorers twice, with 61 points in 1945-46 and 72 the next year.

They played together until Max was traded away by the Hawks early in the 1947-48 season but it's doubtful they ever had a better night than that of December 4, 1941, just three days before the Japanese attack on Pearl Harbor brought the United States into World War II. It was a night of "infamy" for the Montreal Canadiens at the Stadium, the Hawks rolling to a 9-2 victory. Late in the first period, Doug stole the puck from a Canadien, circled the Hawk blue line, then passed to Max. As Max rolled down ice, ragging the puck, the Canadien defenseman on the right bore down on him. Meanwhile, Doug skated down the left boards and yelled shrilly, "Max! Max!" Glancing to his left, Max saw that Doug was in full stride toward the goal, with just one defender to beat. He led Doug with a perfect pass and without breaking stride the man with the puck swung past Canadien defenseman Jack Portland, wheeled in on goalie Best Gardiner, and snapped a wrist shot past him.

That was just the start. Less than two minutes later, with the help of Mush March and Joe Cooper, Doug scored his second goal. In the third period the Bentleys combined again. This time Max faked out goalie Gardiner, while Doug rolled around the defense and skated in on the net for the scoring shot that earned him the hat trick.

Just about 14 months later, on January 28, 1943, the Bentleys and Bill Thoms put on one of the greatest exhibitions of point-gathering ever achieved by a line. The result was a 10-1 rout of the New York Rangers by the Hawks. Max, Doug, and Thoms got 18 points in the game, six of them goals. Max had four goals, all in the third period to tie a record, as well as three assists for a total of seven points. Doug got two goals and four assists. Thoms settled for five assists.

There were many other great nights for the Bentleys, if not for the Hawks as a team. And when Gottselig combined them with Mosienko in 1946 it seemed the ultimate in a line had been achieved. The label "Pony Line" finally stuck, but it was only arrived at after a little experimentation by publicist Farrell. Farrell was thinking about what he had seen after a particularly sparkling exhibition of skating and scoring by the Bentleys and Mosienko. He thumbed idly through a newspaper, then looked up, nodding to a friend.

"I've got it!" he exclaimed. "The Gazelle Line! The fastest thing on feet—the gazelle. The fastest thing on skates—Max Bentley, Doug Bentley, Bill Mosienko. What a natural! I am reading about this gazelle boy down in India—runs 50 miles an hour. Bosh, those Bentleys and Mosienko skate 150 miles an hour. With my failing eyesight, it is getting so I often cannot see them skate by."

The Hawks had other fine players through the 1940's, the most notable, of course, being defenseman Johnny Mariucci, Joe Cooper, and Earl Seibert, the last of whom was selected an All-Star for ten consecutive seasons. Robert (Red) Hamill, Gaye Stewart, Metro Prystal, and Roy Conacher were among the more notable forwards.

Mariucci, 5 foot 10 inches and 200 pounds, had been a football end at the University of Minnesota and didn't forget it on the ice. He was the Hawk policeman of the '40's and was involved in many battles, the most ferocious being a fight with Black Jack Stewart of the Canadiens that lasted a full 15 minutes. Mariucci, after his professional career ended, went on to coach hockey at the University of Minnesota. Ironically, he became later the apostle of clean play and sportsmanship as coach of the U.S. Olympic hockey team.

Despite the sensational feats of the Bentleys and Mosienko, the ruggedness of Siebert and Mariucci, and occasional excursions into the play-offs, the 1940's and early 1950's constituted a grim era for the Hawks. They finished last nine times in a stretch of 11 seasons and in the 21 campaigns from 1940-41 to 1960-61 only once did they win more games than they lost.

The decline may have been due in part to the death of Major McLaughlin on December 17, 1944. Tobin took over the team, purchasing controlling interest for $340,000 August 15, 1946, but his leadership was uncertain and he was continually leaving himself open for second-guessing.

He blamed the Hawks' plight on the refusal of the rival teams to make deals.

Toronto manager Conn Smythe roared back, "The Hawks have had a chance to buy players from us, but Tobin is so cheap that he wouldn't pay 10 cents to see the Statue of Liberty take a swan dive into New York Harbor."

Perhaps Tobin's greatest mistake was his trading of Max Bentley to Toronto on November 3, 1947, for five players: Gus Bodnar, Ernie Dickens, Gaye Stewart, Bud Poile, and Bob Goldham.

"It's the biggest trade in the NHL for a long, long time," president Clarence Campbell of the NHL told a reporter, "and only goes to emphasize the worth of Bentley as a player."

It certainly did, as Bentley played better for Toronto than the five players did for the Hawks, and the team's downturn was more pronounced than ever. Even that usual recourse of management to shore a failing team, changing coaches, didn't help. At the end of 1947 Gottselig stepped up to manager, naming Charlie Conacher, a brother of the immortal Lionel, to coach the team. Conacher lasted to the end of the 1949-50 season, then was replaced by Ebbie Goodfellow, who hung on two years, then stepped aside for Sid Abel, a great Detroit Red Wing player.

Charlie Conacher made his most notable contribution to Hawk history off the ice. Perturbed by a 9-2 beating the Hawks took in Detroit on February 9, 1950, and the felling of Doug Bentley by a Detroit player, he manhandled the referee. Then, questioned about the incident by Detroit writer Lew Walter, Conacher knocked him to the floor. He was fined $200 by the league for the incident.

It took a while for the Hawk's ineptitude on the ice to tell at the gate. The early postwar years were of unprecedented prosperity. The Hawks for a time were hockey's greatest gate attraction, reaching an attendance high of 521,837 for 30 home games in 1946-47 and on February

23, 1947, drawing a record crowd of 20,004 to the Stadium.

Tickets to Hawk games became so difficult to get that publicitor Farrell got an offer from an undertaker for a free burial plot in exchange for the rights to buy a pair. The Stadium press box, reserved for newsmen, was the target of the ingenious, who used involved schemes in attempts to gain admittance.

Farrell didn't let up his guard for a moment. He was tough on intruders. One night he spied a priest in the press box.

"I'm sorry father, you'll have to leave," Farrell told the priest.

"But I have a press pass," said the interloper, "and don't you know who I am?"

"Don't you throw your cloth at me," roared Farrell. "This place is for working press only."

The priest departed but before he disappeared he stopped at the bottom of the stairway and pointed an accusing finger at Farrell.

"You might need me some day," he said and was gone.

At least the priest was a man of peace. The same could hardly be applied to many fans in those days. If possible, they were even rowdier than their sons—and daughters— two and three decades later. Francis (King) Clancy, the great little defenseman of the early days of the NHL, could attest to that. In the early 1940's Clancy had turned to refereeing, and it was his fate to find himself most often in Chicago. One night, as he positioned himself near the boards to watch a face-off, an irate female fan jabbed him in the rear end with a large hat pin. Another night a spectator reached over the boards and took a punch at Clancy's face. The blow missed, but Clancy climbed over the railing to return the compliment. He disappeared into the crowd and in the turmoil it was difficult for the sportswriters, looking down from the press box, to follow the battle.

Immediately after the game the sportswriters ran down to the referee's room to get a firsthand account of the battle from Clancy and to see whether he had suffered any damage. An exuberant Clancy greeted them: "Look! Take a good look at me, will you. There isn't a mark on me."

"Not even a scratch?" asked a hopeful reporter.

"Not one. The guy never touched me. Not a scratch," insisted Clancy.

The reporter sighed in mock disappointment. "That's too bad, King. You're right. Not a scratch. But you have just dashed the hopes of 19,842 Chicago fans."

Opposing players as well as referees often felt the ire of Chicago fans. A near riot was precipitated in the Stadium on November 2, 1949, when three Montreal Canadien players got into a dispute with a number of spectators. A Hawk fan even chased Canadien Ken Reardon across the ice. The 20-minute outbreak was halted by the arrest of Reardon, Leo Gravelle, and Billy Reay and carting them off. After it was pointed out that several of the fans involved in the fracas were hoods, the three Canadiens were cleared. Actually no charges ever were placed against Reay.

It wasn't the last time Reay was to know the ire of Hawk fans. It was in another capacity, however, and quite a few years later that he was again to receive the brunt of their anger and frustration, as well as being lauded to the skies. That later experience was to come only after an extended period during which the Hawk franchise languished and almost died, with attendance in the early 1950's falling to the level of the team—rock bottom.

Tobin, bewildered by what was happening, was able to do little to halt the slide in artistry and finances. He replaced Coach Charles Conacher with Ebbie Goodfellow in 1950-51, wailed about how the popularity of that novelty television was affecting attendance, and began looking for a chance to get out from under.

9

No Place To Go but Up

IT WAS on September 11, 1952, that Tobin officially announced his surrender of controlling interest in the Black Hawks. For a long time he had been beholden financially to the owners of the Stadium, James D. Norris, Sr., his son James Dougan Norris, and Arthur M. Wirtz. Now they stepped to the fore. The elder Norris, who for two decades had owned the Detroit Red Wings, died just three months after taking over the Hawks. The task of rebuilding the franchise fell to his son and Wirtz.

At first the job seemed hopeless, although the rest of the teams in the league banded together to help out the Hawks in a succession of trades. The transfusion actually started in the Tobin regime, and the connections of the Norris family, still in the background, had had a lot to do with it, as they owned Detroit openly while owning Chicago covertly.

In July 1950 a nine-player trade was announced between Detroit and the Hawks. The Wings received goalie Jim Henry, defenseman Bob Goldham, and forwards Gaye Stewart and Metro Prystal. The Hawks received goalie Harry Lumley, defensemen Al Dewsbury and Jack Stewart, left wing Pete Babando and center Don Morrison. A separate deal gave the Hawks Lee Fogolin and Steve Black for Vic Stasiuk. A year later the Hawks bought six players from Detroit for $75,000, the biggest cash deal in NHL history up to that time. They got George Gee, Max Mc-Nab, Clare Martin, Clare Raglan, Jimmy Peters, and Jim McFadden. This brought to 19 the total of former Red Wings in the Hawk organization but failed to make the team a winner like Detroit, which was then the power of the NHL.

Even when Norris and Wirtz took command, prosperity was not just around the corner. With attendance falling to an average of 4,000 a game, it was apparent that the most likely thing around the corner for the Hawks was another city in which to plant the franchise. Rumors that the Hawks were going to move to St. Louis, or even withdraw from the league, became so strong in 1953 that the younger Norris had to remind people that he could run the Hawks for two or three centuries even if they lost $1,000,000 a year.

"I know of $100,000,000 I can put my hands on," he once said. "For sure, there's $200,000,000 around, and I'm probably worth $300,000,000."

Wirtz, although a careful man with a dollar, could put his hands on almost as much. He had been a partner of the elder Norris, who had built up his fortune in grain. The Wirtz money came from real estate, hotel, banking, and railroad interests. But while Wirtz kept a careful eye on things, it was Norris who took the more active part in the Hawks as a sporting proposition.

Norris, in his late 40's at the time, already had gained national fame in sports, as president of the International Boxing Club. His picture appeared regularly on television screens as the promoter of prizefights, until the federal government broke up the IBC as a trust. He also was prominent in horse racing. But his abiding interest was hockey.

"Racing is pure luck," he explained. "In boxing the outcome has nothing to do with the promoter. But hockey—it's a team sport where psychology and desire are half the game."

The other half—as Norris saw it—was money, the funds with which to acquire and develop players. He resolved to pour in whatever money was needed to revive the failing Hawks as a long-term proposition. For the short term, he put pressure on the other clubs to help him out. Detroit did its bit by sending over aging star Sid Abel to coach the Hawks. Toronto's contribution was a four-for-one player deal in which the Hawks surrendered goalie Lumley in exchange for goalie Al Rollins, Cal Gardner, Gus Mortson and Ray Hannigan. The new blood was red enough to get the Hawks into the play-offs in 1952-53 for the first time in seven seasons and the only time in a stretch of 13.

In 1953-54, the Hawks dropped back to last place, winning just 12 games, losing 51 and tying 7. Goalie Rollins, oddly, won the Hart Trophy as the league's most valuable player, apparently for extraordinary gallantry under fire.

Norris, using his influence with Detroit, a team owned by members of his family, persuaded the Red Wings to part with the man he thought could lead the Hawks out of the wilderness—Tommy Ivan. In July 1954, Ivan, who had coached Detroit to six first-place finishes and three Stanley Cups in seven years, was named general manager of the Hawks.

Ivan, then 43 years old, had the perfect schooling required for his job. He was a protégé of Jack Adams, hockey's version of baseball's Branch Rickey, a man who ruled and drove the Detroit Red Wings to success for thirty years (1933-1963). Adams seemed to know everything there was to know about hockey and Ivan leaned heavily on the older man's example.

"Adams is the best thing that ever happened to me," said Ivan, who may have been the best thing that ever happened to the Hawks.

When he came to them in 1954, Ivan faced what seemed an almost hopeless task. His job was to accomplish what a succession of coaches and managers, changing almost every year, had failed to do: find a hockey team amidst the rubble that then was the Black Hawks. Not only had the team won just 12 of 70 games the previous season, but it was bereft of talent. There were only 40 players in the entire organization, and that included a few amateurs scattered in Canada.

"It was very dispiriting," admitted Ivan. "There was a lot of work to be done."

Fortunately, he had never been easy to dispirit. Born in Toronto in 1911, Ivan had set out to become a professional hockey player, but got only as far as a junior amateur in Brantford, Ontario, where a puck shattered his jaw and cheekbone in the 1934-35 season. That ended his playing career.

"But I was never very good anyway," he said, intimating it was just as well he was forced into other channels.

He turned to coaching a junior amateur team, and in 1937 he caught Adams' eye. He became a Red Wing scout and started upon one of the most successful careers in hockey history. He scouted for the Red Wings, then coached Detroit-controlled amateur teams, taking time out for four years of service in the Canadian Army during World War II. After the war Adams sent Ivan to coach the farm teams at Omaha, Nebraska and at Indianapolis, Indiana. At Omaha Ivan coached a youngster named Gordie Howe, who later won some fame at Detroit.

Ivan's success in the minors was so marked that in 1947 Adams promoted him to coach the Red Wings. The appointment was a triumph, the Red Wings winning the Prince of Wales Trophy six times in seven years and taking the Stanley Cup in 1949-50, 1951-52, and 1953-54. Ivan could have stayed on for life as Detroit coach but stepped off a Stanley Cup championship team to take over a moribund Chicago organization.

"I was kind of tired of coaching," he explained simply. "I wanted a crack at managing, a new challenge."

That the Hawks certainly were. Fortunately, Norris and Wirtz gave him what amounted to a blank check to spend in rebuilding the team. It was a check that Ivan was going to have to fill in for $2,000,000—perhaps $3,000,000—before success was in sight, but Norris never blinked. He knew Ivan needed every penny he could spend. What he took over in 1954 was not a hockey team but a home for semi-retired players of uncertain and rare vintage.

For a time Ivan continued the system of wholesale trades in the hope he could slowly lift the Hawks to respectability. In quick succession players such as Bucky Hollingsworth, Johnny McCormack, Frank Martin, Pete Conacher, Ray Timgren, Red Sullivan, Ike Hildebrand, Bill Gadsby, Nick Mickoski, Allan Stanley, Bob Hassard, Tony Leswick, Glen Skov, John Wilson, and Benny Woit arrived on the scene and stayed for varying periods of time. Among the best were wing Litzenberger and defensemen Stanley and Gadsby.

"If we can just improve ourself a little bit with each trade I'll be satisfied," said Ivan. "You pick up a little bit here and a little bit there and maybe it will add up to something better."

On Ivan's arrival, Abel was replaced as coach by Frank Eddols, who struggled without success to lift the 1954-55 Hawks. He was able to squeeze just one more victory out of the team than Abel had been the preceding year, but winning 13 games couldn't lift the Hawks out of last. At least, Litzenberger had proved his value, leading the team with 23 goals. He was to become captain of the Hawks and lead them in scoring three more times, hitting a peak of 33 goals in 1958-59. But despite all of Ivan's machinations, the Hawks remained a haphazard collection of cast-offs and fading stars.

"It was a place where hockey players used to come to finish their careers," said Piere Pilote, the little defenseman who was to join the Hawks a couple of years later as one of the first of a succession of bright stars. "You could learn a lot from the guys we had because they had been around plenty. But they didn't have much left."

Not even the return of Dick Irvin, one of the original Hawks of 1926, helped. After being fired by Major McLaughlin in 1931, Irvin had gone on to a triumphant career as coach of the Montreal Canadiens. In May 1955 Ivan brought him back to coach the Hawks.

"We're going to shoot for third place," Irvin announced. After a valiant struggle the Hawks won six more games than the previous season, yet remained firmly in last place. Irvin's sense of humor was tested to the breaking point. Luckily he was blessed with wit, gaining fame as an after-dinner speaker. Asked once, "What is meant by sudden-death overtime?" he responded: "It's like this: when your team gets the first goal, it's sudden; but when your opponent gets it, it's death." Irvin's humor lasted longer than his health. He was forced to step out as Hawk coach a little more than a year after taking the job.

For a time Ivan both managed and coached, until the burden proved too great. Then in January 1958 he named an unknown, Rudy Pilous, coach. The appointment of Pilous, a hearty, outspoken extrovert, totally without big-league experience, was the culmination of the long-range rebuilding program Ivan had been carrying on below the surface while seemingly running a veterans' rest home in the Stadium.

Ivan had taken the first step in the long-range plan in January 1955, when he purchased the Buffalo minor league franchise for $150,000, chiefly to get young defenseman Pilote, but also to provide a "finishing school" for young players. He had set out to scout and sign promising teen-agers and train them on a chain of farm teams. He built the farm system from "scratch," starting out at the level of sponsor clubs—amateur teams on which the untried youngsters could be developed or discarded. The big league team provided the financing.

The first sponsor club obtained by Ivan was a junior amateur organization at St. Catharines, Ontario, the Tee-Pees, operated by Pilous.

"I remember at the time the Hawks had their eyes on a big fellow we had, a fellow named Elmer Vasko," said Pilous. "Ivan got the TeePees to get him as much as for any other reason."

The move may have been Ivan's shrewdest. From the TeePees came a succession of fine players, including Bobby Hull, Stan Mikita, Vasko, Matt Ravlich, Pat Stapleton, John McKenzie and others.

In Ivan's first years, however, this crop wasn't ready for the harvesting. He was still getting improved material by the simple expedient of trading and drafting, hoping that every time he turned a man over he would get someone better in his place. In this way he picked up a lanky young fellow from the Toronto organization who was to be around a long time. The youngster, who had been touted as another Jean Beliveau but hadn't quite lived up to expectations, was named Eric Nesterenko.

Ivan's efforts began to move the Hawks ahead perceptibly. They won a few more games each year, becoming almost respectable. Then in 1957 he made one of the shrewdest deals in hockey history, one that was to be the foundation stone of the rebuilding. The Detroit Red Wings, furious at forward Ted Lindsay for his activities in forming the first NHL players' association, sold him to the Hawks along with baby-faced goalie, Glenn Hall. Lindsay was to play three years for the Hawks, but he wasn't Ivan's chief target.

"Lindsay was on his way down then," said Ivan. "The man we were after was Hall. We were a long way from developing a goalie of our own."

For the next few years Hall took care of all the Hawk goaltending requirements, playing a record 552 consecutive games in net. And his acquisition signaled the final step in the revival of the Hawks, who now had a bombshell ready to burst into the NHL down at St. Catharines in the person of 18-year-old Bobby Hull. Ivan handed the fuse to Pilous. He decided that combining the jobs of coaching

and managing was an unsatisfactory arrangement. A coach
has to deal with day-to-day matters. A general manager
must look at the long-term picture. Sometimes the two
ways of thinking clash. Ivan realized it would be better
to divide the responsibility.

"We wanted to find someone who was qualified, someone from our organization, who had previous experience
with the players we developed," explained Ivan. "Although
Rudy's coaching experience was limited, we decided he
was the man for the job because of what he had accomplished at St. Catharines."

Pilous, although his forceful personality and school-
masterly approach grated on veteran players, proved an
ideal coach for the youngsters, who now came flooding up
to the Hawks from Ivan's farm system. Within three years,
fortified with the new stars, Pilous led the Hawks to their
first Stanley Cup in almost a quarter of a century. Later
on, as the young Hawks grew older, Pilous' manner was
to antagonize them. His open criticism of his players and
his lack of tact were to set them against him. Nesterenko
was to grumble, "Pilous couldn't coach a girl's softball
team." And his failure to win a Prince of Wales Trophy,
after several near-misses at finishing first, was to disenchant
Ivan, Norris, and Wirtz.

But that was all in the future. In the late 1950's Ivan,
spending millions of dollars of Norris-Wirtz money, developed a farm system stocked with more than 300 players
distributed on 11 teams. The Hawks' future for the next
decade was assured. Ivan had spent well, and Norris and
Wirtz could hardly complain as fans began to flock back
to the Stadium, jamming it as in the halcyon days of the
1940's.

"I had the two most patient bosses in the world," said
Ivan. "Too much can't be said for them. They kept
hockey in Chicago and made the Hawks the team they
are."

Norris' willingness to spend money was never better
demonstrated than in October 1962, when he not only

offered $1,000,000 for a single hockey player, but wrote out a check for that amount to the Toronto Maple Leafs. The player Norris wanted for the Hawks was left wing Frank Mahovlich, who had scored 81 goals for Toronto in the previous two seasons. At 24 Mahovlich was considered certain to become a player in the class of Gordie Howe and Maurice (Rocket) Richard.

What could have been the biggest deal in sports history started out at a party in Toronto's Royal York Hotel on Friday night, October 4, 1962, the day before the annual NHL All-Star Game was to be played. The discussion veered around to Mahovlich, who had scored 48 goals the previous season and was holding out for a big raise from Toronto.

"I'd give one million dollars to be able to negotiate with that guy," said Norris to several Toronto executives. "I wouldn't have any trouble signing him."

"You'd what?" asked Harold Ballard, Maple Leaf vice-president. "You'd give how much to be able to sign him?"

"You heard me," said Norris. "I'd give one million dollars to be able to negotiate with him. One million dollars. But you wouldn't sell him, I guess."

"Every man has his price," replied Ballard.

Excited, Norris pulled Ivan into another room. "How good a hockey player is Mahovlich?"

"Pretty good," said Ivan.

"Worth five hundred thousand dollars?" When Ivan nodded yes, Norris named a higher figure. Ivan blanched, but Norris didn't lift an eyebrow. "I think I can get him. I think Ballard would sell."

He returned to the other room and began bargaining with Ballard. He finally named one million dollars.

"You've got a deal," said Ballard, winking at Maple Leaf president Stafford Smythe to show he could go along with a joke as well as the next man. You get Mahovlich for a million."

Norris pulled out his wallet and counted out ten $100 bills, handing them to Smythe as pledge of his good faith.

"That's a deposit," said Norris. "You'll get the check in full in the morning."

Ballard accepted the $1,000 and he and Jack Amell, a Leafs director, grabbed a scrap of hotel stationery and signed a statement. It said, in part: "We . . . except (sic) $1,000,000 in payment for Frank Mahovlich."

A jubilant Norris told Ivan. "Let's call the wire services in Chicago. We got Mahovlich."

Ivan telephoned Gottselig, now the Hawks' publicity man, to spread the word. Saturday morning's newspapers carried the headlines: "Hawks Buy Mahovlich for Million."

The next morning Ivan took the check for $1,000,000 to the Leafs' offices. But the morning after had brought sobering reflections to the Toronto owners. Smythe hedged: "I will not consider such a deal made at a party." He then called a meeting of the board of directors, and it was decided that the offer had to be "reluctantly declined."

In later years it was often questioned whether the offer of $1,000,000 for Mahovlich had been made in earnest by Norris. It was denounced as a grandiose publicity stunt. Yet it is certain that a check for $1,000,000 was made out and that Ivan attempted to deliver it to the Leafs. In any case it was a grand gesture and an indication of just how strongly Norris felt about the Black Hawks. Unfortunately, the team was never able in his lifetime to realize his greatest desire, to see them finish in first place.

Yet the Hawks did reward Norris with a Stanley Cup and with two players—Bobby Hull and Stan Mikita—whose fame far surpassed that of Mahovlich, before Big Jim died on February 25, 1966.

At his graveside, a colleague paid a tribute that Big Jim would have appreciated: "Norris saved the game in Chicago."

That he did, with the millions of dollars that he did spend and the millions more he would have been glad to spend if it would have helped.

10

The Goal and Mr. Goalie

BOBBY HULL never got the shot away. He hurtled down the ice like a tormented bull, slammed into Detroit goalie Hank Bassen, and lost the puck in front of the net. As Bassen lay dazed in front of the unprotected cage, Ab McDonald, Hawk left wing, pounced on the puck and with the same motion shovelled it into the net. That goal, scored on Sunday night, April 16, 1961, in Detroit's Olympia Stadium, was the most satisfying one the Hawks had achieved in 23 years. When McDonald's shot flew into the net, the red light signalled the culmination of Ivan's efforts during the preceding seven years. No goal was to match McDonald's in importance for another six seasons.

By the beginning of the 1960-61 season, Ivan had shaped the essential framework of the Black Hawk team as it was to stand for most of the following decade. Almost all of the major players who made the Hawks a formidable power during the 1960's were already in uniform.

Most important was Bobby Hull, just 21 years old, already the Golden Jet, a youngster who had scored 39 goals the previous year and was to score 31 during the 1960-61 season. There was also Stan Mikita, only 20, and becoming known in Montreal as Le Petit Diable (The Little Devil) for his aggressiveness. He already was displaying the superlative ability at center that made him Hull's fore-most rival as the game's outstanding player of the 1960's. There was Glenn Hall, 29, the quiet man in the nets, whom his teammates called "The Ghoulie." Hull was at the height of his powers, another Gardiner. There were Pierre Pilote and Elmer (Moose) Vasko, the small and the large, equally superb as defensemen. And there were Kenny Wharram, 27, Bill Hay, 25, and Eric Nesterenko, 26, who were all to play roles far into the future. There were the others—McDonald, Earl Balfour, Murray Balfour, Litzenberger, Tod Sloan, Reg Fleming, Dollard St. Laurent, Jack Evans, and Al Arbour—whose terms with the team were to be more limited but whose contributions in 1960-61 were of major significance.

Ivan and Pilous had put all the ingredients together and their years of work were rewarded at the instant McDonald scored the goal that assured the Hawks the Stanley Cup for 1960-61.

But before McDonald got the chance to score that goal, the Hawks went through a tempestuous regular season, finishing in third place only after a flaming windup that included one of the most spectacular brawls on hockey ice in a decade. The brawl took place in Toronto's Maple Leaf Gardens, starting when Pilote banged Eddie Shack over the head with his stick. That touched off a row that culminated in all the players pouring off the benches to get at each other. Before order could be restored, Murray Balfour chased Toronto's Carl Brewer up the ice, threatening to kill him, and other Hawk players were up in the stands fighting with spectators. It took four policemen to break up the brawl. Referee Frank Udvari collected $725 in fines.

With Fleming, a rugged, aggressive, bottle-shaped forward acting as "policeman," the Hawks literally fought their way into the Stanley Cup semifinals. Montreal won the opening game 6-3, but Canadiens Bill Hicke, Jean Beliveau, and Don Marshall were injured, leading to charges of "dirty hockey" against the Hawks. They weren't at all abashed and bounced back to win the second game 4-3. It was the third game, in the Stadium, that proved the turning point. Montreal's Henri Richard tied the game at 1-1 in the last minute of play. Two overtimes later the score remained 1-1. In the third period, during a Hawk powerplay, Mikita fired from left point and got the puck to Murray Balfour, standing in front of the net. Balfour just wheeled and fired a backhand shot to put the puck through the goalie's legs. The defeat was costly in another way to Montreal coach Toe Blake: he took a swing at referee Dalt McArthur and was fined $2,000.

Montreal, firing 60 shots on Hawk goalie Hall—52 in the first two periods—won the fourth game 5-2 to even the series at two victories apiece. But Hall didn't give them another goal in the series and the Hawks went on to win the next two games to move into the finals against Detroit. They exchanged victories with the Red Wings in the first four games, took the fifth 6-3 and went into the second period of the sixth game tied 1-1. That's when McDonald scored the goal that gave them a 2-1 lead, which was built up to 5-1 by game's end. As the final horn went off, sticks and gloves went up in the air and the Hawks jubilantly lifted Glenn Hall on their shoulders and carried him off the Olympia ice. He was Mr. Goalie and he had brought them the Stanley Cup, the first time since 1937-38.

Since a snowstorm delayed the Hawks' return to Chicago until the next day, they celebrated impromptu in Detroit. In the morning, after they landed at Chicago's O'Hare Field, they got a siren escort downtown, a parade, and a speech from Mayor Richard J. Daley. He described them as the greatest hockey team "ever put together any place in this world."

The same night co-owners Norris and Wirtz pitched a champagne victory party for the players and their wives in the lobby of the Palace Theater. There were many toasts, but there is little doubt the most sincere one was in honor of goalie Hall, who above all the others deserved credit for the team's achievement.

Hall yielded only 12 goals in the six games with Detroit and was almost invincible in the final game. The only puck that got by him was on Parker McDonald's tip-in of a long screened shot by Gordie Howe in the first period.

Hall's sparkling play in the finals, however, was comparatively a let down from the show he had put on in the semifinals against Montreal. What made it all the more remarkable was that Montreal was coming off its fourth consecutive regular season championship. But Hall held the powerful Canadiens, with such scorers as Beliveau, Boom Boom Geoffrion, and Dickie Moore, scoreless for the final 171 minutes and 50 seconds of Stanley Cup play. He concluded the semifinal series with back-to-back shutouts of the Canadiens.

His teammates labelled Hall fittingly "Mr. Goalie" for this and many other feats over the ten seasons he played with the Hawks. He was Mr. Goalie to Chicago from 1957-58 to 1966-67, when he was drafted away by the new St. Louis Blues at the age of 35.

Hall's major league career started with Detroit, where he was selected rookie of the year in 1955-56. He won the Vezina Trophy for the lowest goals-against average in 1962-63 and shared it in 1966-67 with fellow Hawk Denis DeJordy. Later, with St. Louis, Hall again shared a Vezina Trophy, this time with Jacques Plante.

Yet with all this, it is doubtful if Hall ever enjoyed his job. It is certain he didn't in the later stages of his long career.

"You've got to be a little sick to be a goalie," he said, less than half in jest. "The more you think about it the more you wonder."

What "you wonder" is whether it is really worth the money to face the sharp, flying skates, the puck that travels over 100 m.p.h., the bodies that occasionally hurtle into the net to smash a man against the steel ribs of the cage.

And there's the constant tension, the inability to relax an instant—the fraction of a second it takes the puck to fly past the goalie into the net.

"There have been nights when I almost wished I didn't have to go out on the ice," Hall admitted, once commenting: "All I want to do is to stand out in the middle of the 160 acres I've got near Edmonton and holler, 'Damn you! Damn you! Damn you! Damn you!' until I'm good and hoarse and hear the 'You! You! You!' echo back across the field."

It was a way of emphasizing the distaste he had for the crowd noise and other pressures of hockey, the attendant publicity, and the questioning of the sportswriters. This wasn't just a pose. Hall is a shy, quiet man, most pleasant to people who know him intimately but stand-offish to those who don't. His appearance of unruffled calm while with the Hawks was deceptive. He was unbelievably tense, often vomiting during games, before games, and after them. If he suffered an attack of nausea on the ice he tried to control it by breathing deep: "I learned that by watching basketball players on the foul line."

Yet this bundle of vibrating nerves set a record that may be even more remarkable than that of baseball's Lou Gehrig, who played 2,130 games consecutively for the New York Yankees. On November 7, 1962, after 10 minutes and 21 seconds of a game against the Boston Bruins, Hall was forced to leave the ice because of a painful back injury. (He was replaced by young Denis DeJordy.) It was the first time that Hall had been off the ice during either a regular season or Stanley Cup game for the Hawks over more than seven seasons and a string of 552 consecutive games. Hall had played the most demanding position in sports for 31,195 minutes and 33 seconds. He had played despite sometimes severe injuries, despite the constant tension that kept his stomach in turmoil and brought him to the bench on occasion to throw up. He explained his unbelievable tenacity as a case of simply doing his job:

"Sure, there have been times in the last seven years when perhaps I wasn't in condition to play, but making that decision is not my job. My job is to stop the puck. If somebody wants to bench you, okay, but you don't bench yourself. You don't give your job away."

Moon-faced Hall, 5 feet 11 inches, weighing 180 pounds, never gave his job away, not even at the beginning as a 13-year-old in Humboldt, Saskatchewan. As captain of a boys' team in those days, he was faced with a rebellion, when one day the five other boys skated off the ice with an ultimatum to Hall.

"If you want to have a goalie for this game you'd better be it, because none of us is going to get in there," his buddies told Hall. He was faced with a quick decision.

"It was about 10 minutes before game time," said Hall. "So I played goalie that day and kept playing it."

He did, for the next quarter of a century. And so well most of the time that Ivan and Coaches Pilous and Reay, as well as many other hockey experts, rate him as one of the best of all time, ranking not far behind the legendary Gardiner.

Ivan and Reay never faced a more difficult decision than whether to yield Hall or DeJordy in the 1967 expansion draft, when each of the original six NHL teams was permitted to protect only one of its top two goalies. Later, as Hall continued to play well for St. Louis, while De-Jordy descended into mediocrity, Ivan and Reay often were criticized for leaving Hall unprotected.

"It was a difficult decision, but the only one we could make," said Ivan. "After all, Glenn is seven years older than Denis. And we had high hopes that Denis would develop into an excellent goaltender."

Another factor was Hall's reluctance to play any longer in Chicago. Always sensitive, he had been deeply hurt by the fickleness of the Stadium fans, who were quick to boo his occasional failures. Rationally, then, Ivan made the right decision in keeping DeJordy, who had played equally well when he shared the job with the older man during the 1966-67 season.

For half a decade the word that governed the hockey life of DeJordy was "patience," a trait he had to cultivate to an extraordinary degree. For five years he labored in the shadow of Hall. He played his first professional game for Buffalo in 1957, about the time the Hawks got Hall from Detroit. He spent a couple of seasons at Sault Ste. Marie, then three full seasons at Buffalo before playing his first big league game in November 1962, on the memorable occasion when he replaced Hall, who had to leave the ice after playing in 552 consecutive games.

The next two seasons DeJordy became a "press-box goalie" for the Hawks, sitting with newspapermen to watch games. Until the early 1960's, NHL teams were not required to keep an extra goalie in uniform during games, although one had to be standing by in case the regular goalie was injured. DeJordy was assured that watching games from the press-box and being in the nets during practice would help perfect him in his art but he couldn't believe that.

"In practice maybe you keep sharp but you do not learn anything," he said. "A guy will come in, make all the good moves, but when the shot is ready, he does not—well, give it that extra effort. Only in a real game do you learn."

After two years of watching Hall work, DeJordy's thirst for action became overwhelming. On his request he was sent to St. Louis, then a Hawk farm team, where he could play regularly. The next season, 1966-67, the Hawks brought him back and prepared for expansion by using Hall and DeJordy just about evenly. The move was a success. Between them Hall and DeJordy won the Vezina Trophy with a combined record of 2.43 goals-aginst a game. DeJordy worked in 44 games and had a 2.46 average, very close to Hall's 2.38 for 28 games.

At first, Hall was made nervous by having DeJordy around.

"I was afraid I'd suffer by comparison," he said. "But that changed. I decided it would be better to have Denny with me. There was satisfaction in the thought that if I began to go bad Denny would be in our net. Goalkeepers, you know, have a fear of getting stoned eight or nine games in a row. That couldn't happen now. Two bad games and I knew Denny would be there."

Denis was there, especially in working 11½ games of a 14-game unbeaten string early in 1966-67. The Hawks also profited from having two goalies alternating who had markedly different styles of working.

"Glenn is a reflex goalie; I'm more of an angle goalie," explained DeJordy. "I have to move out to cut down the angles. Glenn can stay back a litle longer because he has those great reflexes. I have to move out and stay up. If I go down, that's when I get in trouble."

It was a trouble he was to get into too often after Hall departed and he became the No. 1 Hawk goaltender for the following two seasons. DeJordy never lived up to the promise he had shown in his first years with the Hawks. He was Mr. Goalie's successor but never his equal. It was the Hawks' good fortune—and Ivan's ability to size up talent—that brought them a goaltender in a class with Hall. But that was far in the future; during most of the 1960's Mr. Goalie ruled behind the nets for the Hawks, and much of their success was owing to him.

11

The Accursed

THE MORE successful the Black Hawk players were as individuals in the early 1960's the more frustrating was their failure as a team. It had been easy to laugh off The Curse of The Muldoon in the 1940's and 1950's, when the Hawks were saddled with a collection of cast-offs and mediocrities. It wasn't surprising that such poor teams upheld the supposed prophecy of Muldoon (the first Hawk coach) that Chicago would never finish in first place. Nobody expected the Hawks to do well enough to catch Detroit, Montreal, or Toronto in the years before Ivan embarked on his task of molding a contender for the championship.

After he provided the Hawks with such great players as Bobby Hull, Stan Mikita, Pierre Pilote, Kenny Wharram, and Glenn Hall, as well as others of almost equal calibre, it became a mystery why the Hawks couldn't finish first. Year after year Hull, Mikita, Hall, Pilote, and Wharram were picked on the league All-Star team. Yet year after year the Hawks would make a strong drive for the top only to fade as the season waned and to drop into second or third place.

The Stanley Cup championship of 1960-61 raised expectations for the next season to a peak. And it did turn out to be a remarkable year. Bobby Hull became only the third hockey player in history to score 50 goals in a campaign. (Only Rocket Richard and Bernie (Boom Boom) Geoffrion, both of Montreal, had accomplished it before.) Despite Hull's achievement, however, the Hawks finished in third place. And in the 1962-63 Stanley Cup play-offs, despite an exceptional performance by Mikita, who set a record for most points, with 21 on six goals and 15 assists, the Hawks lost in the finals to Toronto.

The pattern had been set. The Hawks continued to follow it. With what seemed the greatest collection of stars in hockey they finished in second place in 1962-63 and 1963-64, dropped to third in 1964-65, rising to second again in 1965-66.

"They're just a collection of prima donnas," scoffed the critics. "They can't play together. It's every man for himself, trying to make his bonus for goals and assists. They're not team players."

Other newspaper experts and players on opposing teams put it more bluntly: "They haven't got the guts, the heart it takes to be champions."

The greatest collapse of all came in the 1962-63 season and cost Coach Pilous his job. The Hawks carried a solid lead into the final three weeks of the regular season but wound up on the last day a point behind first-place Toronto.

That was all for Pilous, who had lost the confidence of his players and, more important, that of management. Yet the blame was not his. Despite the glittering lineup of big name stars—Mikita, Hull, Hall, Vasko and Pierre Pilote, who for three years running was named the league's top defenseman—the Hawks didn't have the depth of truly fine teams. Their top players had to go all out to keep them in the race and late in the season they were always too worn out to keep up the pace.

Whether or not he was to blame, Pilous was replaced in June 1963 by Billy Reay, then 44, a former Montreal Canadien center, the same man who was involved in a memorable fracas with Stadium fans in 1949. Reay's success in the Black Hawk's farm system and a brief time as coach of the Toronto team had qualified him for the promotion.

Reay and Pilous met by accident at a Montreal race track in the summer of 1963, and the new coach of the Hawks asked his predecessor: "Do you have any advice for me?"

"I sure do," Pilous replied. "Be darn sure you finish first."

The advice was excellent for any coach in any sport, but for a long time it didn't seem that Reay would have any more success in achieving it than Pilous.

Despite the introduction each season of such exceptional newcomers as forwards Chico Maki, Phil Esposito, Ken Hodge, and Dennis Hull (Bobby's younger brother) and defensemen Pat Stapleton, Matt Ravlich, and Doug Jarrett, the Hawks continued to challenge and fail.

Not even Bobby Hull's record-breaking season of 1965-66, when he scored 54 goals to outdistance the achievements of Richard, Geoffrion and himself, seemed to provide enough impetus to reach the top. And the skeptics couldn't be blamed for predicting a collapse in 1966-67 when the Hawks moved into first place at mid-season. It was a familiar pattern; if the Hawks ran to form, they would stay in first until the last week in March, then discover a new way to drop into second place.

Then came the afternoon of March 12, 1967, a sunshiny Sunday when a big young right wing named Kenny Hodge built himself a memory for a lifetime. He built it with a puck that didn't even have time to quiver at his feet after arriving on a pass—Hodge whacked it into the net without hesitation, then jumped three feet off the Stadium ice with stick upraised in the traditional scoring salute of hockey.

"I could live to be 100, and that's one goal I'll never forget," said Hodge. And it's a goal that none of the 20,000 Black Hawk fans who were on hand and saw him score it are likely to forget either—not even after a lifetime of attending games.

That goal and another one earned Hodge an extra bottle of champagne in a wild locker room scene after the game, the most elusive victory in Black Hawk history. It was a 5-0 triumph over Toronto that set all doubt at rest and clinched the Hawks' first regular season championship since they entered the league in 1926. The Curse of the Muldoon finally had been laid to rest. As the Hawks celebrated their first Prince of Wales Trophy with a wild champagne party in the locker room right after the game, they recognized that no man had earned the victor's vintage more than had Hodge, who slapped in the first pair of three goals in the game's opening period and assisted on the third one. Plenty of credit went to others, too: to Bobby Hull, who scored the 48th of the 52 goals he put in during the 1966-67 season; to Lou Angotti, a little buzz-saw center, who repaid the loud affection of his fans, roaring, 'Lou! Lou!' every time he appeared on the ice, with a pair of third period goals; and to Hall, the goalie who once again came up with a shutout in a vital game.

But it was right wing Hodge, just 22 and destined to win further fame playing for the Boston Bruins, who got the big goals on that unprecedented day in 1967. The pair he got in the first period made the game a downhill run the rest of the way for the Hawks.

"I knew we were up for this one," he laughed, the champagne bubbling down his handsome young face as Mikita playfully poured a bottle on his head. "You could feel it before the game—everybody was r'aring to go. It was team effort all the way. With all the help I've had this year, you can't help playing good. And lately everything just has been falling into place for me. You've never seen so much team effort and desire. You'd have to be blind not to see it."

A man would have had to be blind, indeed, not to note the desire and team effort that Coach Reay had instilled into the 1966-67 team. Without it, a title wouldn't have been possible despite the superlative play of the great stars Bobby Hull and Stan Mikita. The previous unsatisfying seasons had shown that. Ice hockey, like basketball, baseball, and football—or any other team game—required total effort from all the players on the roster.

A veteran observer, who had seen the Black Hawks try and fail for decades, took note of this: "The simplest analysis of success is that the Hawks played this one as a team, not as individuals. It is not suggested here that the Hawks were in the past individual glory-seekers. It's just that Billy Reay finally found all the parts to make the whole piece of machinery run."

The "machinery" was at its smoothest in the title-clinching game. One of its best parts was Hodge, a solid 6 feet 2 inches and 200 pounds, with pleasing hockey meanness that served him well that Sunday, particularly on his second goal for which he had to battle Toronto's rugged defensemen.

Center Phil Esposito, who like Hodge was to rise even to greater fame at Boston, centered the puck from the right face-off circle. Hodge and Bobby were battling Maple Leafs for the puck in front of the goal mouth.

"Phil's pass was perfect—right in there," said Hodge. "Bobby just kicked it with a skate and it came right across to me. The net was open and all I had to do was whack it in."

Hodge did that, to Toronto goalie Terry Sawchuk's right, at 15:12 of the first period, less than four minutes after he had scored his first goal of the game—only his sixth of the season. That one came as he hovered at the goal's right post and snapped in a perfect pass coming from Esposito in the left corner. Hodge then rounded out his inspiring first period by snapping a pass from right wing to defenseman Pat Stapleton on the left. Stapleton instantly led Bobby Hull, coming down the middle. Sawchuk had no chance to stop Hull's backhand shot.

The Hawks now had a three-goal lead and could afford to play defensive hockey through a scoreless second period. Goalie Hall withstood several furious Toronto charges. But in the third period, Angotti, who knew only one direction —every which-way—put the game completely out of reach for the Leafs. At 5:57, Angotti snapped a face-off puck away from Leaf Dave Keon with such velocity that the disc slipped through Sawchuk's glove for a goal. And at 18:06, Angotti capped a powerplay by taking a lead pass from Kenny Wharram and driving a slapshot past Sawchuk from far out on the right side.

Those two goals doubled Angotti's scoring production for the entire season and earned him an ovation from the crowd, surpassed only by the one that hailed the entire team at game's end. The crowd's reaction to his play deeply moved Angotti, misting his eyes with emotion. It was a special tribute to Angotti's exceptional hustle, not only in that game but during the entire season. It was recognition of a player with limited talent but unsurpassed determination.

"I think it had an effect on everybody," said the happy little man. "But to be honest, we've got a real good hockey team and being part of it gives me more of a lift than anything else. The only way you can play on a hockey team as great as this is to play all out. When I'm on the bench I want to get in there and play as well as I can because that's the way everybody is playing. I have to. You have to play hard to play on this team at all."

Angotti's words were the capsule comment on the Hawks of 1966-67, a team that won more games (41) than any Hawk team before it and scored more goals (264) than any team in NHL history up to that time. For 40 years no Hawk team had come more than close to a Prince of Wales Trophy, until that Sunday afternoon when the Hawks whipped Toronto and clinched the NHL championship.

Not even the Hawks' subsequent failure in the Stanley

Cup semifinal series, in which they lost four games to two
to Toronto, could diminish the magnitude of their achievement. As a matter of fact, success during the regular season probably contributed to failure in the play-offs.

"Maybe winning the league championship took a lot out
of them," said Reay. "We concentrated on winning that
and when it came to the play-offs we gave Toronto the best
shot we had but it was not there. It just was not there."

Perhaps it wasn't there because of late-season injuries to
Bobby Hull and to Doug Mohns, the high-scoring left wing
of the Scooter Line, as well as the weariness of the others,
who had put so much effort into winning the league championship.

Yet on that joyful March 12, 1967, there could have
been no suspicion of the disappointment ahead as the
Hawks celebrated their triumph by drinking champagne
and by dunking into the showers Reay, Ivan, and other
club officials, including Bill and Mike Wirtz, the sons of
owner Arthur M. Wirtz. The drenched Ivan dripped
happily after escaping from his exuberant players. But
even as he praised Coach Reay for the achievement of the
dream he couldn't help thinking about Big Jim Norris,
who had poured so many dollars into the attempt to achieve
this very goal, yet had died a year before it was attained.

"You've got to give Billy a lot of credit," said Ivan. "If
we missed the title before because it wasn't a whole team,
then you've got to give Billy the credit for making it one.
For me, it is a great personal satisfaction, greater than anything I've had in hockey. I just wish Jim Norris had been
here to see it. The Wirtzes have been wonderful but Jim
wanted it so much."

But then the Hawks as a team wanted it too. They won
that 1967 championship because they wanted it enough
to go all out to get it. Nobody wanted it more than
Mikita, the little center, who was Bobby Hull's only rival
as the finest hockey player of the 1960's. Hull has the
glamor and the big scoring punch. After all, he is the only

man in hockey history to score 50 or more goals in four different seasons. But Mikita has the finesse, which also earned him recognition. Both in 1966-67 and the following season he won an unprecedented three individual NHL trophies: the Art Ross, as the league's scoring leader; the Hart, as the most valuable player; and the Byng, for sportsmanship. Without question, Mikita, at 26, was in his prime in 1966-67, a center worthy of comparison with all the great ones. He scored 35 goals and made a record 62 assists for 97 points, thus tying the record Bobby Hull had set the previous season.

Undeniably, the Hawks' triumph was the result of team effort, but just as surely Mikita was the key man in the march to the top. If lesser players like Angotti and Hodge contributed their share by playing all out, Mikita contributed more than his share because along with his unsurpassed will to win went great talent. In the final analysis, much can be done with desire, a great deal can be accomplished by skill, but nothing can beat the combination of both the will to win and exceptional ability.

It was the Hawks' good fortune that Mikita possessed both qualities in great abundance and combined them as never before in the year of final achievement of the long elusive goal.

12

Stan the Man

THE ORGAN should have played "Tales from the Vienna Woods," but instead of a waltz the accompaniment was the frenzied roar of the Satdium crowd as Stan Mikita figure-skated in and out of Montreal Canadien ice.

Mikita had shaken the puck loose from a Canadien along the boards in Hawk territory, then had charged up ice until two Montreal defensemen double-teamed him. He spun out of their grasp, picked up the loose puck again and wove back and forth across Canadien territory as Montreal's finest helplessly watched. The crowd jumped to their feet, roaring their appreciation of the way Mikita had killed off the last 30 seconds of a Black Hawk penalty.

The cheers also thanked Mikita for sparking the Hawks to a 5-0 victory on November 24, 1966, in the early part of the drive toward their first championship. He had scored one goal and assisted on another. The manner of the first goal was remarkable. Mikita slid by the Montreal net with two Canadiens hanging onto him as Kenny Hodge cut loose a slapshot from 50 feet away. Falling backward, Mikita swiped frantically at the rebounding puck and slapped it into the net for a goal. Even Tommy Ivan, who had watched Gordie Howe score from unbelievable angles, was amazed.

"That goal he got, only he could have gotten!" exclaimed

an awed Ivan. "Falling on his tail! A great second effort. Only *he* could do it."

"I was off balance," admitted Mikita. "I was knocked back and I just shot for the net on the chance the puck might go in. It surprised me when it did."

He didn't shoot for the net on the other goal, in which he played a part. He took a pass in the corner from Hodge, who was inside the blue line along the left boards. Mikita barely touched the puck, flicking it to linemate Kenny Wharram, who was driving in on the net on the right. Wharram snapped a wrist shot past the goalie.

In killing the penalty, shooting the "impossible" goal, and making the perfect assist, Mikita demonstrated the balanced offensive and defensive talents that make him one of the greatest players of hockey. For a time Mikita's varied talents earned him the ranking as the sport's No. 2 player, behind teammate Bobby Hull, universally ranked as No. 1 in the late 1960's. And there were many people who thought Mikita was No. 1.

Maybe it would be best to take Mikita at his own valuation, for no man can surpass the measure he has taken of himself and few live up to it. But if Mikita skates in the shadows of Bobby Hull—or anyone else, including Boston's Bobby Orr—he does not acknowledge it, and what others say cannot diminish the brilliance of his play. Those who labeled Mikita No. 2 to Hull's No. 1 got a fitting answer from Mikita: "Show me the man who ever considers himself No. 2 in anything."

That is a creed and Mikita lives by it—what's more, he plays hockey by it. In his first ten full seasons Mikita was selected on the first-string NHL All-Star team six times and on the second team twice. During the same period Bobby Hull annually, without contest, was selected as the first-string All-Star left wing. In the matter of honors they ran neck and neck in the 1960's, although this did not prove one or the other man was superior. It took a brave man to choose between them at the time, although Boom

Boom Geoffrion, while New York Ranger coach, made a selection.

"Bobby excites the crowd more but Mikita is the better all-around player," said Geoffrion. "They're two different types, of course. Stan works the puck. Bobby can shoot it from center ice and score."

Coach Reay, naturally enough as the boss, would never make a comparison. "I just get the biggest thrill of my hockey career in watching them both play," said Reay. "I consider myself lucky to be coaching a team that has two such great players."

What is significant in all this is that Mikita, a small man at 5 feet, 9 inches and 165 pounds, rates a valid comparison with Hull, who has averaged more goals scored per season than any other player in history. There is no question at all on another point, that Mikita was the best center in hockey for several years, perhaps of all time.

"I've seen most of the good centers who have been around for the last 25 years or so," said Reay. "I have to say I have never seen a better center. Maybe some could do one thing better than Stan, like skating faster or shooting harder. But none of them could do all the things that a center has to do as well as Stan does. And very few of them came close to being as smart as he is. That's his greatest assest. He's smart. He's about the brightest hockey player I've ever seen."

Reay finds it difficult to single out one of Mikita's skills as more noteworthy than another, saying: "He does everything well, he's a natural athlete. He has a very good shot. If he was bigger, he'd be the best body-checker in the league. He throws a terrific body-check, but you hate to use him in that way because he might be hurt. He's a good playmaker, a good skater, and has good reactions. He sizes up the situations fast. He's a hard-nosed hockey player. One of his biggest assets is that he has got a lot of pride."

It is this pride that makes Mikita formidable to opposing

goalies, because they always must beware of his tremendous capacity for second effort. One of the most spectacular goals of his career came as he slid on his belly past the goal mouth, flailing at the puck with the stick extended in front of him.

Goalie Glenn Hall, still a close friend and a teammate until he was drafted by the St. Louis Blues in the NHL expansion of 1967, knew just what he was up against in Mikita. "The guy has such tremendous reflexes and so much talent that he can change his mind in mid-stride when he's skating or shooting," said Hall. "And believe me, a guy who can do that drives goalkeepers nuts. You think you have their moves figured, and they come up with something else before you can adjust."

Mikita admitted to this fierce pride, to a belief in expanding mental as well as physical potential on the ice: "Your mental attitude is the most important thing in this game," he said. "Ninety per cent of the guys in this league shoot the same, skate the same, stickhandle the same. The only difference is in mental attitude. You have to have the desire or you don't do anything. A lot of times a guy will think, 'Aw, I don't feel like it, let the other guys do it.' That's when they get beat.

"Sure, there are times when I feel like that myself. I remember before a Pittsburgh game in December of '67 I went to the locker room feeling rotten and I didn't even want to put my skates on. I had to push myself. Yet that night I scored four goals."

It is this ability to override the worries and problems of the moment that sets Mikita apart. He didn't feel like playing, yet he scored four goals, a rare feat for even the greatest players. Never were his abilities to disregard physical problems and mental weariness, as well as to improvise tactics (as Hall noted) better displayed than in the final game of 1967-68. Mikita went into that concluding game against the Detroit Red Wings at the Stadium with a sore back and a challenging task. He was leading the scoring race by just a point. Both Phil Esposito, traded to the Boston Bruins the previous May, and Gordie Howe, then in his 22nd year with Detroit, had a chance to catch or pass him. Mikita had 84 points on 39 goals and 45 assists going into the game, Esposito had 83 points and Howe had 81. What made Mikita's task even more challenging was that he knew at the end of a futile first period that Esposito had scored a goal in a game between Boston and Toronto that was being played concurrently.

"With Esposito playing on home ice and on a line with Eddie Shack, who likes to get his goals in Boston, I was worried," admitted Mikita. "I was shaky all through the first period."

Shaky or not, Mikita picked up a pair of assists in the second and third periods as the Hawks battled back from trailing 3-0 to Detroit after the first period. Mikita's assists came on goals by Scooter Linemates Wharram and Mohns as the Hawks caught the Red Wings at 4-4 midway in the third period. But then a short-handed goal by Detroit's Dean Prentice at 14:46 gave the Red Wings the lead again. And it was still possible that at Boston Esposito might be picking up the points to pass Mikita in the scoring race.

The pressure was on, but just 12 seconds after Prentice's goal, Mikita demonstrated both his hockey smartness and his ability to rise to the occasion. With a strange move he sewed up the scoring title and tied the game at the same time. At right point he took a pass from Mohns and from long range just flipped the puck toward Detroit goalie Roger Crozier. The puck took the bounce Mikita evidently had hoped for, and shot to the left past Crozier into the net. Mikita's goal was similar to one Camille Henry of the New York Rangers had scored against Montreal in a game televised nationally earlier in the day. Mikita admitted that Henry's goal had given him the idea of trying for a similar shot if the opportunity arose. He had been watching the game with teammate Bobby Schmautz.

"Bobby and I were talking about Henry's goal before this game started," said Mikita. "I said, 'Nine years I've tried that shot in practice and I've never done it yet in a game.' When you shoot the puck like that it has to start dipping and then bounce either this way or that"—and he motioned to the left and right. "Believe me, I've really been working on that shot, but it's still a lucky one."

Certainly, luck had something to do with that puck going into the net for a goal, but so did Mikita's fierce determination to finish first in the scoring race, even if it meant gambling on a freak shot. The gamble was justified. As it turned out, Mikita had put enough room between himself and Esposito and Howe. And after the game, in which he had met the challenge and won his second straight scoring title and fourth in five seasons it was Howe, the great competitor, who came up with the tribute: "Stan deserved the glory—he didn't back in." It was a tribute worth savoring and no doubt Mikita still savors it, for it came from the best of sources in Howe, who scored more goals than any other man in hockey history. Howe knows what it's like to want to be No. 1 just as Mikita does.

It is a quality that makes it difficult for Mikita to be anything less than No. 1, either as an individual player or as a part of the team. The 1968-69 season, when the Hawks plunged into sixth place, was an unrelieved disaster for Mikita, although he again got 97 points to match his own career high. This was good only for fourth place in the scoring race, topped by Phil Esposito with an unprecedented 126 points, but what really hurt was the team's showing.

"I don't think I've had such a bad year," said Mikita. "A lot of guys I know would be glad to settle for 97 points. But what difference does it make when the team doesn't win? It takes the joy out of it."

That's why Mikita can never be No. 2, because in his heart he is always No. 1, maybe because he's afraid of being anything less.

Mikita has an older brother, George, a fact that has a great bearing on how he became one of hockey's greatest players. When George was born in 1938 in Sokolce, a little town in Czechoslovakia, the proud parents received a telegram from the baby's uncle and aunt, Joe and Anne Mikita, who lived in St. Catharines in Ontario, Canada.

"My uncle put it—kiddingly or not, I don't know—in the telegram that 'When the next one is born, I'm going to come over and get him,'" said Stan Mikita. "I didn't know about this until many years later when I visited my mother and other relatives in Czechoslovakia." The fulfillment of this pledge was long delayed by World War II. Stanislav Gvoth (who was to become Stan Mikita on adoption) was born May 20, 1940, in Sokolce, the son of a textile mill worker.

Eight years after Stan's birth, in 1948, Joe Mikita made good on his promise. With his wife Anne he visited Sokolce and persuaded the Gvoths to let them adopt their younger son Stan and take him to Canada. It was a difficult, heart-breaking decision for the Gvoths to consent to parting with their son. But post-war conditions were difficult in Czechoslovakia. The parents saw their son would have a great advantage in life by growing up in the relative peace and prosperity of Canada.

Mikita, then eight years old, vividly recalled the day of parting.

"I was lying in bed in another room of the house and I got hungry and yelled to my mother, asking for some bread and jam," said Mikita. "They had discussed with me the possibility of going to Canada, and they were talking about it with the Mikitas in the kitchen part of the house when I hollered for the bread and jam. My mother yelled back, 'No,' because she thought I shouldn't have the bread and jam. I thought she was saying no to my going to Canada and I began to cry. Everybody else started to cry, too."

Despite the tears, the difficult decision was made to let the Mikitas take Stan with them to Canada. The little boy was happy but soon discovered it wasn't as easy as all that to leave his parents.

"When my aunt and uncle finally were taking me to the station in Prague, I wondered what Canada would be like and I was eager to go. But when I got to the station and saw that the train was ready to pull out and my mother and father were going to be left behind, I wrapped my arms around a pole and cried. Every inch of the train ride I plotted to jump off and go back to my mother and father."

If Mikita had been able to foresee what lay immediately ahead of him he might well have jumped off the train. Still, the toughness and determination that were to make him such an outstanding athlete were developed in the streets of St. Catharines, where survival with dignity was not easy for a growing boy.

"Children at that age can be very cruel to anyone who is new or different," said Mikita. "I found that out right away. The other kids used to call me D.P. (for displaced person) and made it sound like a cuss word."

From some of the youngsters he learned even more derogatory terms than "D.P." and "foreigner," but he also picked up such English words as "puck," "stick" and "goal," words that were to have great meaning.

"I think I picked up English in six months," said Mikita. "It's a little easier to learn a language when you're a kid in the streets, playing hockey and other games. I'd learned to skate a little in Sokolce, but I had never seen a hockey stick until I came to St. Catharines."

Evidently, he knew instinctively what to do with the stick.

"I'll never forget my introduction to hockey," he said. "We both were about nine years old, me and this kid who lived down the street. We read in the newspaper about the Canadian Legion—a war veteran's group—sponsoring a hockey league, sort of like the Pony League in baseball. Anyway, it was supposed to be for kids 12 to 14 years of age, but I told the people who signed me up that I was small for my age. He said he'd check with my dad. I ran

STAN THE MAN 87

all the way home and told Dad to say I was 12 years old if anybody called to ask."

Apparently the deception worked and now all Stan had to do was worry about making one of the teams in the league. Ironically, he made the team called the "New York Rangers." He was the smallest player in the league, but one of the toughest. He already had learned that hockey was no game for sissies while participating in a scrimmage in the street.

"The first thing I did when a kid tried to skate past me was to whack him across the shins with a stick," laughed Mikita. "That started a dandy fight and I was pretty badly beaten. I guess I've been fighting to get along ever since."

He learned from the start to go all out or else.

"We had an instructor, Vic Teal, who knew a lot about hockey and made sure we picked up everything we could," recalled Mikita. "He was tough. We had to do things right or he would hit us hard with a broom on the shins. I remember that broom very well and appreciate now what it did for me."

Of course, he needed more than a whack with the broom to help him learn the game of hockey. He needed equipment and ice time. His dad supplied the first, and odd jobs, such as sweeping up the rink and picking up litter, provided the money for the rest.

"Funny, you look back on it now, how things were, what was really important then," he mused. "When I got into the league it was the first time I had a pair of skates that I didn't have to tie on to my shoes. After a couple of years my dad said since it looked like I was going to stick with the team he'd buy me a pair of good ice skates. He paid $23 for them, which was a lot of money back in 1952. I'll never forget how proud I was of those skates."

The skates, the broom, and his inborn skill prepared him for a hockey career that he didn't even realize existed until he was 16 years old. He didn't know until then that people actually were paid for playing hockey.

"That's when I saw my first professional hockey game,"

he said. "Honest, I was 16 years old, but in hockey I was still a 9-year-old kid with his first pair of real ice skates."

Mikita was a fast learner, however, not only in hockey but in other sports as he progressed through grade and high schools. He played a game of bantam lacrosse in 1954 when he was 14 and scored eight of his team's 12 goals. One afternoon when the TeePees, his Junior B hockey team, were returning from a trip, the bus let Mikita off at Saltfleet where the senior team was playing football. It was half-time and Mikita got in uniform, then went out and scored a touchdown to lead the team to victory.

By this time the Black Hawks already were scouting Mikita, whom they had placed on their "list" as the rules of the day permitted when he was only 13 years old. They watched carefully his progress, which was almost meteoric. At 18 he was being touted as the best Junior A hockey player in Canada, scoring 31 goals in 1957-58 and leading his team to a league championship. During the 1958-59 season the Hawks brought him up to the major league team for the three-game trial then permitted under the Canadian amateur rules.

The first team Mikita faced in the Stadium was the Montreal Canadiens. And the first time he stepped on the ice was to face-off against Jean Beliveau, the Canadiens' formidable center. Mikita won that first NHL draw. On the same shift, he also took the puck just inside the Montreal zone, sent Doug Harvey, the all-time great Canadien defenseman spinning with a beautiful feint, and drove in on goalie Jacques Plante.

It would have made a fine tale if Mikita could have scored on that first drive, but Plante turned the shot aside. In the other two games of the trial Mikita picked up only a single assist. He was returned to St. Catharines but he had convinced Manager Ivan and Coach Pilous of his potential. The next year he was signed by the Hawks.

"I got a two-year contract for $8,500 a season from the Black Hawks, and I was very satisfied with it," said Mikita. "I thought it was very fair at the time."

Since, the pay scale has gone up considerably, reportedly to around $60,000 a year as is only proper for a player who has led the league in scoring four times and has won both the most valuable player and most sportsmanlike conduct awards twice. This second award, the Lady Byng, came as something of a surprise because Mikita during his first seven years in the NHL was known for his aggressiveness. For six seasons he led the league's centers in total penalty minutes.

"If you give Stan a little jab, he reacts immediately," said Allan Stanley, a veteran defenseman who played on several teams. "Most players will wait for a chance to retaliate but Mikita will give it right back to you in the same motion. And he can be ornery himself."

Though still no patsy, Mikita has learned self-control. He knows that he can't score from the penalty box, that he has to stay on the ice to be valuable to the team.

"With a wife, three kids and a mortgage, I just can't afford all those fines I was picking up for misconduct penalties," Mikita joked, but added the warning: "Not that I've reformed that much. I'm not going to let anybody run over me. But a family man has to be more careful."

There was a serious undertone to that statement. In 1963 Mikita had married Jill Cerny, an intelligent, dark-haired girl who was secretary to a U.S. Congressman. By 1970 the Mikitas had three children and lived in a colonial-style house in Elmhurst, a Chicago suburb.

Like most athletes today, Mikita is well aware that some day the big money from hockey won't be rolling in anymore, that it is important to plan for that day.

"I may not have known much about money when I started, but I've learned a lot since," said Mikita. "I've read about all those champions in sports and the big stars and their big money, and how they ended up walking around broke. I don't want that to happen to me."

In order to make sure his future would be provided for, he has branched out, particularly in the developing and manufacturing of hockey equipment. He designed the helmet that he and a number of other NHL players wear. He is connected with a hockey stick manufacturing concern, and developed the curved stick that has become so popular in recent years.

"I'd like to have a white collar job when I retire," he said. "I'm not interested in going back to St. Catharines. I like the Chicago area and have a lot of close friends here. Maybe, after I retire, I'd like to take an active part in community affairs."

Those could include politics. Mikita, a Canadian citizen, in 1968 affirmed his decision to remain in the U.S. by taking out his citizenship papers.

As mellowed as Mikita has been by the passage of years and the resultant maturity (judging by the Lady Byng Trophies for sportsmanship), he still can be riled up by one subject—the recurring rumor there is jealousy and ill will between him and Bobby Hull. He is also weary of the endless comparison of their skills and value to the Hawks. Perhaps his words on that reveal as much as anyone else's opinion of him what sort of man he really is.

"I've been playing on the same team as Bobby since we were in high school together for a while in St. Catharines," said Mikita. "And I get as big a kick out of watching him play hockey as anybody else does. I'm just glad we are on the same team. I'd hate to play against him. Besides, he helps us win games and that puts money in my pocket.

"When I first came to Chicago and walked into the dressing room, he came over to me and put his arm around me. He took me in and we lived together for a year and a half. We've been in business together. We are different types of players, and I can see as well as anyone what Bobby can do. Bobby has the type of personality that allows him to stand and sign autographs after losing a game, but I am not built that way. I will walk away, and I can hear what people are saying about me.

"Maybe that's wrong, but that's Stan Mikita."

ABOVE: Major Frederic McLaughlin, first Black Hawks owner, with star goalie Charlie Gardiner (left) and right wing Mush March.

BELOW: Defenseman Roger Jenkins gives Gardiner a ride around Chicago's Loop in a wheelbarrow to celebrate the Stanley Cup victory of 1934. At left, with pipe, is defenseman Lionel Conacher.

UPPER LEFT: Johnny Gottselig, one of the finest stickhandlers of the 1930s, was an outstanding left wing for more than a decade. He was with the Black Hawks for more than thirty years, serving as coach, manager and publicist after his playing career ended.

UPPER RIGHT: Harold (Mush) March, the little 5-foot, 5-inch right wing who starred for 15 years at right wing, clears the puck out of a corner in a 1944 game. Behind him, defenseman Earl Seibert has just checked Montreal's Toe Blake into the boards.

LOWER LEFT: The "Goalie Nobody Wanted," Alfie Moore, demonstrates just how he stopped the Toronto Maple Leafs to help the Black Hawks toward the 1938 Stanley Cup. Legend has it that Moore was found in a bar and pressed into service for the game that turned the playoffs around.

ABOVE: Seldom has hockey seen a faster skating, higher scoring line than the combination of the Bentley brothers and Bill Mosienko, who starred for the Hawks in the mid-1940s. Mosienko (left), Max Bentley (center) and Doug Bentley formed the famous Pony Line.

ABOVE: Johnny Mariucci took the turns with plenty of speed and power. Mariucci, a former football end at the University of Minnesota, threw his weight around on the ice, too. The defenseman was a noted "policeman" for the Hawks in the 1940s.

LOWER LEFT: Ed Litzenberger was the Hawks' best scorer and captain in the late 1950s. Here, in 1957, he is presented a trophy for leading the team in scoring by Ted Engstrom of the Standby Club, a group of Hawk fans that annually honors the players.

LOWER RIGHT: Bill Tobin (right), who succeeded McLaughlin as the team's owner, confers with publicist Joseph C. Farrell in 1950. The Hawks in those days were making news, but seldom the kind to gladden an owner's heart.

ABOVE: For a decade Glenn Hall ruled the nets for the Hawks, at one stretch appearing in 552 consecutive games without being relieved. He became known as Mr. Goalie and is ranked with Gardiner as one of the finest goalies of all time.

BELOW: It's one of the happiest moments in Hawk history, as (left to right) forward Reg Fleming, Coach Rudy Pilous and goalie Glenn Hall arrive in Chicago on April 17, 1961, after the team won its third Stanley Cup by defeating Detroit the night before.

ABOVE: A frequent sight in the 1960s: Ken Wharram (No. 17) scores against Montreal goalie Gump Worsley with help from Stan Mikita (No. 21).

LOWER LEFT: An even more frequent sight: Bobby Hull slams the puck past Detroit goalie Roger Crozier after a pass from Chico Maki (No. 16).

LOWER RIGHT: No doubt about it! The million dollar check for Toronto's Frank Mahovlich is in Hawk general manager Tommy Ivan's hands. But Toronto rejected the offer.

ABOVE LEFT: Bobby Hull and Phil Esposito (No. 7, later with Boston) were on the same side in this stick-swinging melee with New York's Jim Neilson and Wayne Hillman in 1966.

ABOVE RIGHT: A whole covey of Montreal Canadiens can't stop Stan Mikita from scoring this goal in a 1966 game.

BELOW: Ken Wharram (left), Stan Mikita (center) and Doug Mohns formed hockey's outstanding trio of the 1960s, the Scooter Line.

ABOVE: Pierre Pilote's greatest fame was as a rushing defenseman, but the little man could also throw a pretty mean bodycheck as he demonstrates on Detroit's Nick Libbett in 1968 game. Pilote was captain of the Hawks during the mid-1960s and for three seasons running (1962-63, 1963-64 and 1964-65) was awarded the Norris Trophy as hockey's best defenseman.

OPPOSITE ABOVE: Glenn Hall got plenty of help to earn his title as Mr. Goalie. Here Pat Stapleton (No. 12), Hawk defenseman and Pilote's successor as team captain, moves in to clear away the puck as New York's Bob Nevin (No. 8) awaits pass from Phil Goyette in 1967 game.

LOWER LEFT: Tony Esposito, the new Mr. Goalie, gets set to make the stop on Detroit's Frank Mahovlich (No. 27) that Hawk coach Billy Reay called the greatest save he had ever seen. The stop, on March 26, 1970, set up a 1-0 Hawk victory on the way to the championship.

LOWER RIGHT: Keith Magnuson, (right) demonstrates the heavy bodychecking style that made him a favorite of the fans in his rookie 1969-70 season.

It's a beautiful sight for Black Hawk owner Arthur M. Wirtz and Captain Pierre Pilote as they admired the first Prince of Wales Trophy ever won by the team in March 1967. It was the culmination of forty seasons of effort.

WILLIAM WIRTZ   BOBBY HULL

TONY ESPOSITO

DENNIS HULL

DOUG JARRETT

CLIFF KOROLL

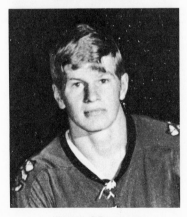

KEITH MAGNUSON

CHICO MAKI

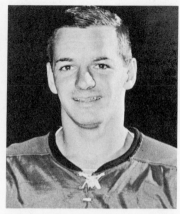

JIM PAPPIN   PIT MARTIN

STAN MIKITA   ERIC NESTERENKO

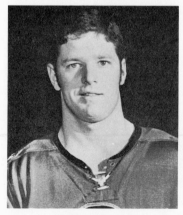

GERRY PINDER   KENNY WHARRAM

13

The Scooter Line

VICTORY in hockey often belongs to the swiftest, always to the deadliest, and there was lightning on ice when Ken Wharram, Doug Mohns, and Stan Mikita skimmed its surface as a unit. The three men formed hockey's most famous scoring combination of the 1960's, the Scooter Line.

Johnny Gottselig, who has seen them all since the late 1920's, doesn't hesitate to put the Scooters in their prime in a class with the greatest lines of hockey history.

"It's as good a line as I've ever seen," said Gottselig. "It compares favorably with such great lines as the Kraut Line that Boston had in the late 1930's and the line Detroit had in the 1950's with Gordie Howe, Ted Lindsay, and Norm Ullman. That Mikita is as great a stickhandler and center as I've ever seen—a marvelous playmaker."

Mikita's skills as a playmaker were complemented by the ability with which right wing Wharram, a dart across the blue line, and left wing Mohns, the trailer, were able to carry out the pattern plays that lead to goals. It was precision skating and maneuvering that made the Scooters so effective, although to the unknowing it appeared merely that the three men were geniuses at improvisation.

"You know, the funny thing is that everybody thinks we're magicians or something of that sort, when all we really do is to make the obvious plays," Mikita remarked.

"We don't do anything unorthodox or surprising. We just keep skating and each of us always knows where the other guy is going to be."

It sounds simple—just skate. Of course, it helped if you could skate as fast and as expertly as Mikita, Wharram, and Mohns could. And it helped that they practiced together by the hundreds of hours and spent as many off the ice discussing tactics and mistakes, and setting up patterns and plays. It helped that they could pass to a predetermined spot on the ice and be certain that a linemate would be there. No, as Mikita said, there was no magic, merely perfect teamwork among the Scooters and almost a sixth sense telling them what each man would do and where he was going to be at any given moment in an offensive rush.

The Scooters did their work swiftly but not silently. To locate one another during attacks on the enemy net they did a lot of yelling. As soon as a man got free for a shot he shouted the nickname of the linemate with the puck. Wharram was "Whip," Mikita "Kita," and Mohns "Mohnsie."

"If you shout once," explained Wharram, "it means you think you have a little time. But if you're in a scramble you yell twice, 'Kita! Kita!' Then he knows he has to rush."

To a casual observer hockey seems like a haphazard game, a scramble on the ice with improvisations, with reflex action replacing plays, but it was not like that with the Scooters.

"We talk over what we are going to do in certain situations," said Mikita. "We may be sitting around having a beer, and we get out a piece of paper to figure out something new or different. Then we'll try it on the ice in practice. That way we know pretty well what to expect, where each of us is going to be, depending on the situation."

The Scooter Line had been in existence for several years before Mohns, a veteran defenseman who had been with Boston for 11 seasons, came to the Hawks as the result of a trade in the summer of 1964. Until then Ab McDonald, a big (6 feet 2 inches and 195 pounds) forward was left

wing with Mikita and Wharram. The Hawks traded Mc-
Donald and brawling forward Reggie Fleming to Boston
for Mohns, whom they intended to use as a defenseman.

Without knowing it, manager Ivan had made the trade
that was to bring the Scooter Line to near perfection. With
McDonald gone, Coach Reay tested several left wings with
Mikita and Wharram, but none of them seemed to fit in
with the swift pair. Meanwhile, Mohns suffered a broken
foot early in the 1964-65 season and while he was sidelined
the Hawks replaced him with a young defenseman, Matt
Ravlich, who played very well. The success of Ravlich
eased the need for Mohns on defense. But the Hawks still
had the problem at left wing on the Mikita line and Mohns,
although a defenseman, had been a formidable skater and
shooter with Boston. One season, although strictly on defense, he scored 20 goals to tie the league record for production on the back line.

"Mikita and Wharram weren't going too good," recalled
Mohns. "They had tried several young players at left wing
on their line but none of them seemed to work out. I un-
stand that Mikita finally went to Reay and suggested that I
be put there. Billy was reluctant to do it because he was
satisfied with my play on defense. But the club was going
so bad that I guess Billy was ready to try anything."

Mikita had noted Mohns' powerful skating and great
ability in bringing the puck out of the defensive zone. He
had a hunch "Dougie the Diesel" would be a perfect match
for the line. He was right.

Mohns contributed size (5 feet 11 and 175 pounds) as
well as solid checking ability and a "heavy" slapshot to the
Scooters, who had great agility and breaking speed in right
wing Wharram (5 feet 8 and 160 pounds) and playmaking
skill and cunning in Mikita (5 feet 9 and 165 pounds).

It took a while for the three men to merge their skills as
well as they were to do at their peak. Mohns had to shelve
his defensive thinking, which came instinctively after 11
years on the back line.

"Sometimes we would rush up and make a pass to

Mohnsie's side," said Wharram, "and he would be moving back. I'd ask why and he'd say that we had left an opposing forward free and he wanted to back us up. He would be right, of course, but that's cautious hockey, the kind you see in Stanley Cup play-offs. It's not really our regular style and we had to get him to thinking more in terms of offense."

As Mikita put it: "We're not a checking line, we're a forcing line. We make the plays and let the other guys worry about checking us."

Despite this emphasis on attack, as Reay pointed out often, the Scooters were also a superb defensive line, the best on the Hawks. Less goals were scored against the Hawks when they were on the ice than were scored against the other units.

"Having Mohns out there is like having a third defenseman," said Reay. "He gets back very quickly and is a very good checker.

Nevertheless, the main task of the Scooters, as Mikita emphasized, was to score, and few lines in hockey history were more productive in goals and assists. In the peak season, 1966-67, the Scooters scored 91 goals (Mikita getting 35, Wharram 31 and Mohns 25) and the line accumulated a total of 222 points, just four short of the record. For five consecutive seasons, beginning in 1964-65, the Scooter Line produced 20 or more goals a year from each of the three men, a balanced output seldom matched in hockey over such an extended period. Even in the final season of the Scooters, 1968-69, they came up with 82 goals (Mikita and Wharram each getting 30 and Mohns 22).

The studied teamwork of the Scooters made them a perfect combination with Bobby Hull and a strong rushing defenseman like Pat Stapleton or Pierre Pilote, both of whom shot well from the points, as a powerplay unit.

A typical example of their concerted play occurred in a 5-0 victory over the Boston Bruins during the 1966-67 season. With a powerplay going, Pilote started the rush from behind the Hawk net, moving down ice and shoving the puck ahead to Mohns on left wing. Mohns went into a corner with the puck, then slapped it out to Wharram behind the Boston net. Wharram faked a pass to Mikita, near the goal mouth, then slid the puck back along the boards to Hull at left point. Bobby, drawing a foe toward him, then slid the puck to Pilote at the other point. Pilote got the puck to Mikita in front of the Boston goalie, Ed Johnston. That was the end of the beginning. Mikita made a move as if to shoot, then paused as Johnston lunged forward. Another fake and Johnston was off balance. Then a shot and the puck passed through the goalie's legs.

Perhaps the ultimate in hockey firepower was reached in a game against Toronto, when the 1966-67 Hawks were operating a powerplay and the foe drew an additional delayed penalty. On a powerplay in the third period Mikita carried the puck into the Toronto zone. The Leafs, in their usual rough style at that time, clutched and jostled every Hawk that came near them. Ron Ellis grabbed Mikita, but Stan spun out of his grasp. Wharram took the puck and was cross-checked by Brian Conacher. "Whip! Whip!" yelled Mikita, and Wharram passed the puck to him. Allan Stanley then boarded Mikita and, to his surprise, a penalty was called.

In such a situation the whistle didn't stop the action until the Leafs got possession of the puck—and the Scooter Line wasn't about to let them do that. For 45 seconds the Scooters controlled the puck, sliding it from one man to the other. Meanwhile, goalie Glenn Hall had come off the ice to be replaced by an extra forward, Bobby Hull. Finally, with everything set, Mikita passed the puck to Hull, who was soaring down the middle directly toward the net. Bobby fired right up the slot for a goal, made possible only by the superb puck-handling of the Scooters.

Such combined effectiveness is achieved only by years of playing together. Wharram and Mikita were linemates for a decade, until "Whip" was forced to retire from hockey by a heart ailment just before the 1969-70 season started.

Wharram, born in 1933, was a Hawk for 11 seasons, not counting early trials going back to 1951. He was an excellent skater, perhaps the fastest man in the NHL for short bursts, and had an exceptional "patented" shot from about 30 feet out on the right side. It was good enough to put him high on the all-time list of scorers with 252 goals. His peak year was 1963-64, when he scored 39 goals and won the Lady Byng Trophy. He was small, but more than compensated for that with hustle and skating skill.

"My speed helps overcome what some might consider to be lack of size," said Wharram. "By keeping on the move all the time with my head up I don't give the defensemen time to set me up for solid checks. Also, when they do hit me, they usually get just a little piece and not enough to ride me out of the play entirely. I try to go all out all the time when I am on the ice. You only get out of a sport what you put into it, and I owe it to my teammates and myself to give my all."

It was a sentiment applicable to all three Scooters as a unit, and Mohns and Mikita continued to prove its validity after Wharram was gone. Mohns went back to playing defense early in the 1969-70 season, and Mikita was provided with two new linemates, left wing Dennis Hull and right wing Cliff Koroll, both of them big men. And the Scooter Line is no more.

But as Coach Reay said when the Scooters were in their prime: "They're unbelievable. As good as any line I've ever seen."

That they were.

14

The Look of a Goal

BILL HAY glided toward the Toronto goal, long smooth strides eating up the ice, eyes occasionally flickering toward quickly moving Stan Mikita at his right.

Nearing the net, Hay faked out two Toronto defensemen, and pulled goalie Terry Sawchuk forward, legs slightly spread, crouched in expectation of a shot. As Sawchuk glanced to his left at the decoy, Mikita, Hay snapped a wrist shot toward him. The puck shot between Sawchuk's pads, then took a peculiar loop up and out of the net. The red light that signals a goal didn't go on. The Hawks protested bitterly but the goal was not allowed. Hay couldn't believe it.

"I put the puck right between Sawchuk's legs and then it looped out," said Hay. "It had to be a goal. He had come out to protect the crease. I had him head on and if the puck went between his legs I don't see how it could have hit the post. I tell you, Sawchuk gave up on it. He had the look of a goal on his face. He knew it had gone between his legs and that there was no way in which it could have hit the post."

However, the goal judge insisted the puck had failed to cross the goal line and referee, Bill Friday, upheld him. Friday hadn't seen the shot. He had been calling a penalty on a Toronto player at the moment Hay took the shot.

That was the "phantom goal" of 1967, which may well have cost the Hawks the chance to add the Stanley Cup to the Prince of Wales Trophy. Without that goal, the Hawks had just a 3-1 lead in the fourth game of the Stanley Cup semifinals at Toronto on April 13, 1967. Before the final horn sounded, Toronto had narrowed the margin to 3-2 and the Hawks had to fight for their lives to take the game and even the series at two victories apiece. The effort was costly. It took too much out of them and they lost the next two games to end the season disappointingly, although they had won the league championship.

Yet the goal that didn't count showed once again the importance of Hay and the other Hawk penalty killers that year. They had stolen the puck from the Toronto power-play unit to turn a defensive assignment into an offensive opportunity.

This kind of theft was frequent with the 1966-67 Hawks and never more so than when Hay and Eric Nesterenko, an exceptional penalty-killing pair, were on the ice. Two seasons earlier, Nesterenko assisted largely by Hay, set a league record with six short-handed goals.

As Reay frequently noted, the importance of defensive forwards Hay and Nesterenko was inestimable. Yet when the 1966-67 season opened Hay wasn't on the team. Although only 30 years old with plenty of hockey ability left, he had retired after the 1965-66 season to pursue his career as a geologist with an oil company in Calgary, Alberta.

Midway through the next season the Hawks, who had led the league in much of the early going, staggered and dropped behind the New York Rangers. It was clear to Ivan and Reay that they had to get a center for the third, or checking line. They also needed a seasoned player to team up with Nesterenko as a penalty killer. Bobby Hull and Mikita had been sharing the job, but the increased work was affecting them offensively.

Ivan's search for a center became so desperate that he

even made an offer to Toronto for Red Kelly, a great player but then 39. When Toronto refused to deal, Ivan called on Hay in Calgary, urging him to join the team. Hay was reluctant, but finally consented to return.

"I came back because the Hawks told me I could help them," said Hay, "and I felt I could. Tommy Ivan told me this team had a chance to win the first regular season championship for Chicago in 41 years, and I wanted to help if I could."

Hay's return was a tremendous stimulus to the Hawks. They won the first game in which he played, lost the next, then went on a 15-game unbeaten streak to virtually wrap up the title. Hay and Nesterenko made the perfect penalty-killing unit. Both were tall (Hay, 6 feet 3 inches and Nesterenko, 6 feet 2 inches), were experienced, and had the skating skill and deceptiveness required of defensive forwards.

"Hay and I have been playing so long together that we don't even have to holler to each other," said Nesterenko. "We sense what we're going to do, where we are going to be. It's impossible to explain, but it's something that can be acquired only after years of playing together!"

Hay was also an offensive threat. He was rookie of the year in the NHL when he came to the Hawks in 1959-60, winning the Calder Trophy. He scored 18 goals while playing on what was exuberantly called "The Million Dollar Line" with Bobby Hull and Murray Balfour. Hay hit a peak of 23 goals in 1963-64 and contributed seven in the 36 games he played to finish out the 1966-67 season and his career.

Rudy Pilous, his first Hawk coach, once summed up the skills of the quiet, efficient Hay.

"He has got a tremendous reach, for one thing," said Pilous. "He uses the longest stick permissible—73 inches. And he has strong arms. He can edge the puck past the other guy, which is why so few of them are stolen away from him. He also has good instincts. His instinct tells him when there are guys alongside him or behind him. When he comes up the ice he's looking straight ahead. He's deceptive that way. But his mind is working. As he's coming in, he may have three different plays in mind."

Reay, Pilous' successor, also thought highly of the man called Red.

"Bill is consistent," said Reay. "He doesn't give you a couple of brilliant performances and then tail off. He'll make the right moves, the big ones that help a team win. And most important of all he's smart."

Hay's contributions off the ice may have been even more important than those on it. He was the natural leader of the Hawks. Though Pilote was the team captain, it was Hay the players looked up to and respected, whose advice they accepted without question. He was quiet but when he spoke it was with penetrating wit.

When the 1966-67 season ended, Hay, having accomplished his task, retired for keeps. He rejected a generous offer from the St. Louis Blues, who had drafted him from the Hawks as part of the NHL's expansion to 12 teams.

Hay's longtime partner Nesterenko provides a contrast in hockey styles. He is a swooper, a roamer on the ice, almost unpredictable, richly deserving of his many nicknames, among them "Ghost," "Elbows," "The Blanket," and the "Thinker."

Nesterenko's skating style is deceptive because of his long, loping strides and the way he leans, almost hovering over the ice. As a youngster in the Toronto system in the early 1950's he was considered to have the makings of a super-star. But by the time he came to the Hawks in 1956 it was clear his defensive skills were predominant. In speaking of him, Ivan remarked:

"Nester has just about as many good moves as anybody. And with those long legs he can change pace very deceptively. He is an exceptional skater and, the amazing thing about him, he seemingly improves with age."

Nesterenko, born in 1933, bore out Ivan's remark. Each

year he seemed to get better, and played exceptionally well at the age of 36 when the Hawks won their second Prince of Wales Trophy in 1969-70. He has never been a big scorer, although he produced 20 goals in 1957-58. But his defensive value has never been in question, and he was just as great a penalty killer working with Chico Maki as he had been with Hay.

15

The Perfect Mesomorph

THE TENSION had been building up for more than a week, and expectation was electrifying the crowd of more than 20,000 crammed into the Stadium on March 12, 1966. In every mind was the question, "Is this going to be the night?"

During the warm-up before the game with the New York Rangers, Bobby Hull fidgeted with the new sticks he was testing by firing pucks toward the net. From time to time he shook his head and frowned. Just before the warm-up he had received a shipment of sticks from the factory. They were curved a little differently than his usual model. They didn't feel right. Nothing felt right. The usually relaxed Hull was almost snappish, his normal amiability strained to the breaking point.

It was almost unendurable. The pressure should have been off days before. The period of waiting for each of the previous three games had seemed interminable. And the disappointment when one after the other ended without Hull—or even the Hawks as a team—scoring a goal was shattering. Would this night be the same?

As Hull flicked his practice shots on net, at the other end of the ring Ranger goalie Cesare Maniago was calmly fending off shots his teammates were throwing at him. His tall body seemed perfectly relaxed as if no thought of what

was at stake that night had entered his head. But he knew
—he had to know. The newspapers had been headlining
the question for weeks, the magazines, radio and television
were full of it—"When will Hull get his 51st goal?"
Maniago had to hope it wouldn't be this game. It would be
no disgrace but there were better ways for a goalie to get
his name in the record books than by giving up a historic
goal.

The build-up had started with a goal ten days before, a
picture goal that underlined Hull's finesse in contrast with
most of his other goals, the product of his brute force, his
awesome strength.

That goal, his 50th of the season, had come in the 57th
game on the schedule for the Hawks against the Detroit
Red Wings on March 2 at the Stadium. It could have
been chalked up on a blackboard, the pattern was so
perfect, it was such a masterpiece of timing and teamwork. Mikita had started it out, bursting down the middle
of the ice, across the red line and the Detroit blue line,
then passing to Wharram, who was slashing diagonally
across from left wing.

"Bobby gave me a holler," said Wharram, "As I was
cutting across I picked up Stan's pass, heard Bobby and
threw the puck back to him."

Hull had been criss-crossing behind Wharram, coming
from right wing, and he picked the puck off the ice just
a dozen feet away from Detroit goalie Hank Bassen.

"I fired a low wrist shot on the goaltender's left, just
inside the post," said Hull. "I'm always enthused when
I score a goal, but never more than that one—that's one
I expect to retrace over and over again. I think it took a lot
of pressure off me."

How wrong he had been! But at the moment of achievement it hadn't been apparent. He was so overjoyed that as
hundreds of hats, paper cups, and other tokens of esteem
floated onto the ice, while the fans gave him a standing
ovation for 10 minutes, he skated over to the east end of

the Stadium and stepped into the stands to kiss his wife, Joanne. He felt he owed her that.

"It has been hard on her, too," he said. "I guess I've been tense and frustrated and maybe I've taken it out on my family at times."

His tension and frustration lifted momentarily when he achieved that 50th goal of the season, matching his own high of four years before and that of Rocket Richard and Bernie Geoffrion in the past. Those three were the only men ever to score 50 goals in a season and now Hull had done it twice. Now there was a chance to go beyond that, to set a record shared with nobody else, to achieve something no other player ever had done, to reign alone as the greatest scorer in the game's history. All these things had to be crowding into Joanne Hull's mind as she stood up to applaud No. 50. She had been a fan like all the rest of those around her for the moment. She had jumped to her feet with excitement as almost 200 feet away Bobby had snapped the puck past Bassen into the net.

For a moment, emotion got the best of Joanne. "I stood up and applauded," she said. "All of a sudden tears came to my eyes. It's the first time I've cried over a goal. I was so glad to have it on home ice for the home fans. They were so thrilled and they appreciated it so much."

She was unaware of it just then, but she was to appreciate No. 51, the record-breaker, even more. At first, right after No. 50, both she and Bobby were certain it would come in the next game. "The monkey is off the back now," said Bobby. But the Hawks were shut out in the next game. And in the one after that. Bobby became snappish. As his wife started speaking one day he turned on her. "Don't talk to me," he said.

When the Hawks, unbelievably, were shut out for the third game in a row, Hull became even gloomier. He searched for an answer. Several weeks before he and Hawk equipment manager Don (Socko) Uren had pleaded with the hockey stick manufacturer to put an extra curve in the blade of the sticks. Bobby had been using the curved sticks for years. The theory is that the curved blade imparts spin to the puck and causes it to dip sharply, like a baseball sinker pitch, before it gets to the goalie. Mikita is credited with being the first modern player to use a curved stick regularly. But Bobby's stick has a blade that is sharper, less rounded than Mikita's.

Just before the March 12 game with New York, Bobby received a batch of the new-style sticks. Those were the ones he was testing in the warm-up. Perhaps they would bring him No. 51. But by game time he wasn't sure.

"I could tell they weren't right in the warm-ups," he grumbled. "I wasn't shooting right."

He really wasn't. It became clear as the game started. Bobby just wasn't having any luck that night. He had his chances, but Maniago had no trouble handling his shots. Either Bobby wouldn't get enough wood on the puck or he would be sadly off target. The first period ended in frustration without a goal for Bobby. The second period vanished and it looked like this wasn't to be the night after all. Maniago was too much for Hull. Even the fact the Hawks were trailing 2-1 in the game as the third period became six minutes old wasn't nearly as disappointing as Hull's failure.

When the referee nailed a Ranger player with a penalty, giving the Hawks a powerplay opportunity, the fans failed to be roused beyond a half-hearted murmur. After all, it clearly wasn't Bobby's night. There was no help for it. He'd just have to wait until the next game. The fans' doubts turned to certainty as Reggie Fleming of the Rangers intercepted a pass off Hawk Bill Hay's stick. But Fleming didn't get full control of the puck and Hawk Lou Angotti was able to contest him for possession in the defensive zone. At Angotti's left, Hull was uncoiling, beginning to move up ice. Angotti got a skate on the puck, booted it to Bobby, then sprinted toward the bench.

Still in Hawk territory, Bobby got the curved blade of

his stick on the puck and began barrelling up mid-ice. As he crossed the Ranger blue line he squared off for a slapshot. Goalie Maniago moved out to cut down the angle. As he did, Nesterenko cut in front of him. Screened by Nesterenko, Maniago got only a bare glimpse of the puck, powered by the full force of Hull's explosive slap and moving at more than 110 m.p.h. It was past him into the net before he could move.

It was No. 51, a new record!

As the red light flashed on, the crowd exploded with a roar of delight, again littering the ice with hats, confetti, scoreboards, newspapers, and hot dog wrappers. Hull, while skating toward the east end to kiss Joanne again, bent down to pick up one of the sillier hats and placed it on his head at a jaunty angle. That drew another roar from the crowd, surpassing even the one that had greeted the record goal. Angotti, the little utility forward who had gotten the play underway with his kick, was overwhelmed by his part in the big moment. "When I'm 65, I'll sit around and tell my grandchildren how I got an assist on Bobby Hull's big goal," he laughed. "I'll tell them how I helped him score while I was sitting on the bench. That's right. That's where I was. I kicked the puck over to Bobby, then skated to the bench and sat there watching as he went up by himself and scored."

Angotti treasures that moment but it's certain Maniago does not. (Coincidentally, he was the Toronto goalkeeper against whom Geoffrion scored his 50th goal for Montreal in 1961). He was even a little miffed at Nesterenko's part in aiding Hull on the goal, and not just by screening the shot. "Nesterenko lifted the blade of my stick and the puck went under it," Maniago explained.

The Hawks went on to win the game 4-2, although Hull didn't score again. He did get three more goals before the season closed, for a total of 54—a record almost matched the next year when he scored 52 to help power the drive toward the championship. And, after a "slump" to

44 goals in 1967-68, came another record, 58 goals, in 1968-69.

It is certain Maniago had nothing to be ashamed of in yielding that historic goal to Hull. After all, over the years dozens of other goalies have failed to withstand Hull's explosive charges up the ice and the booming slap-shot from as much as 95 feet away. He is the only player in history to have scored 30 or more goals for 11 consecu-tive seasons, 40 or more in six different campaigns and 50 or more four times.

Hull, in his prime, was the fastest skater in hockey, traveling at 29.7 m.p.h. without the puck and 28.3 m.p.h. with it. His slapshot has been timed at 118.3 m.p.h., about 30 m.p.h. faster than that of the average player. He can flick even a wrist shot at 100.7 m.p.h. His strength is another great asset. At 5 feet 10 inches and 195 pounds, he has been called the "perfect mesomorph" by physiologists.

"Bobby's the strongest forward in the league," said Leo Boivin, a veteran defenseman. "You try to get him to go over to the boards but it isn't easy. He's like a bull. You hit Hull and bounce off of him. He explodes on you. He's so fast he's hard to keep up with, and so strong you can't push him out of the way if you catch up to him, and so tricky it's hard to hit him clean."

In recent seasons, as Mikita has perfected his skills as a center and young Bobby Orr has come along with Boston to become the superstar of the seventies, Coach Reay has sidestepped the interminable discussion of just who is the greatest and whether Mikita or Hull has been more valu-able to the Hawks. But Reay tipped his hand early in 1965, more than a year before Hull first crossed the 50-goal barrier. Said Reay:

"He's the greatest hockey player I've ever seen. In my time I played against Maurice Richard and Gordie Howe, and I say Bobby is better than either of them. If he avoids injuries, he'll break every record set by Richard and Howe.

He has everything you want in a hockey player—tremendous strength, speed, color and stamina. He has got size and a tremendous shot, and he loves the game."

Reay emphasized that his respect for Richard, a former teammate, merely enhanced his admiration of Hull's skills, explaining:

"Richard was an explosive scorer. He was a fanatic once he crossed that blue line and came in on the goalie. He'd get that wild look in his eyes. They'd 'light up' like two burning lumps of coal, and he would act like a madman until he got his shot on or in the net. But he wasn't as strong as Bobby. This fellow has tremendously powerful arms and shoulders."

Hull's wrists measure nine inches around. His forearms measure 13½ inches around, and his biceps 15½. These are measurements worthy of a heavyweight boxing champion.

Reay continued: "In his prime Howe could do more things right than anybody else—skating, shooting, scoring, and thinking. But Bobby is a combination of Richard and Howe. He has the explosive potential of Richard and the strength and durability of Howe. He can skate faster and better than either one, and he shoots harder. Howe has more finesse than the Rocket had or than Hull has now. But Bobby will acquire more finesse as he gets older."

The charge against Hull's claim to standing as the greatest player in hockey history has been based on the very contention that he lacks finesse. In commenting on Hull, Richard the Rocket made the same charge, denying that Bobby is the best player of all time, or even of the moment.

"Not any more than I was," said Richard humbly. "I scored a lot of goals but there were a lot better players." Then he added, "There may be 25 better stickhandlers in the NHL than Hull, but Bobby has a great thing going for him, the thing that puts the puck in the net."

Of course, putting the puck in the net is what the game is all about and nobody ever has matched Hull in that regard, not even Richard or Howe, not on a goal-per-game-played basis. When Hull reached the 500 goal level mid-way in the 1969-70 season he had played far less NHL games than either Howe or Richard had when they achieved the same distinction.

For durability and the will-power to play despite serious injury, Hull never has been surpassed. With a shattered nose that impeded his breathing, Hull scored three goals in a Stanley Cup semifinal game with Detroit that the Hawks lost 7-4 on April 7, 1963. But his greatest test came in the 1968-69 season when he suffered a broken jaw on Christmas Day, missed just one game, and played six weeks with his jaw wired while he was forced to drink his blended food through a straw. All he did during eighteen games in those six weeks was to score 10 goals.

When the wire came out of Bobby's jaw and the protective helmet with a faceguard that obscured his vision came off his head, brother Dennis Hull predicted: "Watch Bobby come alive. He's going to be like a bird just freed from a cage."

Dennis was right. In the first 14 games after getting rid of the wire and helmet, Bobby scored 19 goals. Then he went on to reach a total of 58 for the season, despite having spent six weeks sipping food more suited to a baby than an athlete and suffering pain each time he was jolted on the ice.

It is one of the greatest feats of all sports history. It is as if Babe Ruth, Roger Maris, Jack Nicklaus, Johnny Unitas, or Wilt Chamberlain had produced their finest seasons while crippled with injuries. They didn't and probably couldn't have done it—yet Hull did.

Whether Hull, young Bobby Orr, Howe, or Richard is the greatest hockey player ever is a subject for debate rather than a fact that can be established. The only certainty is that Hull—chosen NHL Player of the 1960's in a national poll—would have a lot of votes in Chicago and that he could round up a plurality in his native Canadian province of Ontario.

"It was either the cement plant or hockey for me," Hull

once joked, and there might have been more than just a speck of truth in that.

Not too many years ago, Point Anne, Ontario, a little town of 500 people situated 100 miles east of Toronto, was notable only for its cement plant. Today it has new distinction. In one of the most prominent places in town stands a red-white-and-blue billboard proclaiming: POINT ANNE, BIRTHPLACE OF BOBBY HULL, WORLD's GREATEST HOCKEY PLAYER.

Bobby Hull was born on the cold winter night of January 3, 1939, the fifth of 11 children of Robert Hull, Sr., a cement factory foreman. He weighed 12 pounds at birth and the doctor who delivered him joked to his father: "The only difference between you and your son is that he doesn't eat so much."

Robert Hull, Sr., was a fair hockey player himself in his youth, playing on amateur teams in Belleville, a small city close to Point Anne. Like his son, the elder Hull was a fine skater, but his greatest asset was his stick-handling ability.

"I used to marvel at the way he could move up and down the ice with the puck glued to his stick," said Bobby.

The father's physical strength was possibly even greater than his son's. Reputedly, Robert, Sr., a 240-pounder, could lift the front end of a car.

Point Anne is in hockey country, and all the Hulls learned to skate even before they were of school age. Bobby was no exception. Two older sisters, Maxine and Laura, strapped skates on him when he was four and pushed him onto an outdoor rink built by the Canada Cement Company, his father's employer. Once put on the ice, Bobby could hardly be dragged away from it.

"I went back every day and skated until I was exhausted," he said. "I would get up in the morning, stoke fires, put up the water for the porridge on the stove, toss in the salt and head for the ice to skate."

Bobby admitted that it took him a little time to get his

footing on the ice, but he improved quickly—and no wonder!

"I used to skate all morning and afternoon, and only came home for meals. After dinner, I always went out again, and Mum would have to send my sisters out to bring me home to bed."

This devotion to skating, the essential skill of hockey, was a major ingredient in the making of a great player, but the handling of strength and stamina did not come just by chance.

"When I was eight years old," said Bobby, "I started going out into the woods near Point Anne with my grandfather. I chopped down trees with an ax, and that developed my arm and back muscles. I also walked to and from school four miles a day, and during the winter I shoveled snow from morning till night."

The snow shoveling wasn't just to clear driveways, it had an even nobler purpose.

"I was usually one of the first ones out for a game of shinny, and it was up to the first arrivals to clear a skating area," Bobby explained.

All this physical exertion, as well as his Canadian heritage, had a predictable effect. By the time Bobby was eight years old he was "rippling with muscles," recalled a childhood friend. The muscles and the heavy skating stood him in good stead in the games of shinny, a sort of rough-and-tumble hockey with perhaps twenty kids of all ages rushing about on the ice. Bobby learned to shoot and protect himself, but developed a bad habit of holding on to the puck rather than passing it.

At this time his father began to spend many hours on the ice with the boy, paying special attention to developing his stick-handling and passing.

"Let's try it again, Robert," the elder Hull would say. "Keep your head up. If the stick blade is angled properly, the puck will feel right on it."

Dad Hull, like most fathers, would become impatient

with his son at times, but he persevered until he had taught Bobby puck control and how to handle the stick so the puck wouldn't slide off when he took a hard pass. By the time Bobby was 10, he was ready to compete in organized hockey.

Canada has seven levels of hockey competition, ranging from Peewees, through Bantams, Midgets, Juveniles, Junior B's, Junior A's and Professionals. Bobby skipped the Peewees, competing immediately as a Bantam, and even as a Midget and Juvenile with much older boys.

"He used to play hockey practically all Saturday morning," said a friend. "Some mornings he'd score 25 goals in four different leagues."

Bobby's official affiliation was with the Bantam Kiwanis Red Wings in Belleville. He was fortunate in having a good coach named Dan Cowley and even luckier in having a father who took an interest in registering him for the team and making sure he got to the rink. Within a year Bobby captured his first newspaper notice. An item in the *Belleville Intelligencer* said, "Bob Hull stole the eyes of the early morning railbirds."

Bobby stole the eyes of a most important early morning railbird, Bob Wilson, a scout for the Chicago Black Hawks. Wilson came to the rink early one day to look over a player in a later game. Then Wilson saw Bobby Hull! That was enough. Wilson later said he knew immediately that Hull would make it in the NHL. Whether Wilson thought this or not at the time, he was impressed enough to take Bobby's dad aside and get permission for the Black Hawks to draft the boy. From that moment on, at the age of 11, Bobby was the "property" of the Black Hawks. He continued to play hockey at home until he was 14, then the Hawks sent him to their Junior B farm team at Haspeler, Ontario, 170 miles from home.

It could have been an unnerving experience for so young a boy. Bobby was boarded with a strange family, went to a strange high school and learned to play hockey with a group of strangers—all for $5 a week. But he liked it, and his mother and father visited him often. During four years, from 1953-57, the Hawks moved Bobby from town to town, from high school to high school. He attended four schools, was briefly expelled from one, and didn't graduate from any. But he did learn hockey.

When Bobby was 16 the Hawks sent him to their Junior A team, the TeePees at St. Catharines. The coach was Rudy Pilous, the man who later was to lead the Hawks to a Stanley Cup. Hull didn't satisfy Pilous, at least not as a center, the position he still was playing. Pilous accused Bobby of "hogging the puck," and tried to nag him into passing off more to his wingmen. When nagging failed, Pilous shifted Bobby to left wing.

"A good center should pass off to his wings," said Pilous. "If you can't, we'll put you on left wing where you can carry the puck enough to satisfy both of us."

The move stuck. Pilous had found the position at which Bobby was to gain fame. Unfortunately, Bobby didn't foresee this at the moment. He rebelled. He left the team and went home to Point Anne. Pilous retaliated by suspending him. But Bobby's father talked the boy into returning to St. Catharines, where an intermediary arranged a peace meeting with the angry coach. Bobby was reinstated—as a center.

He finished the 1956-57 season at St. Catharines with 33 goals in 49 games and got an invitation to work out with the Black Hawks, who were going to train there the next fall. Bobby had little thought or hope of making the Hawks at the age of 18 but dutifully attended the workouts, meanwhile returning to school and playing football.

On a momentous September day in 1957 Bobby worked out on the ice in the morning, played football in the afternoon and was just in the middle of dinner at his boarding house when the phone rang. The Hawks were playing a pre-season game against the New York Rangers that night in St. Catharines and they wanted Bobby in uniform.

It was a nervous moment for the boy of 18, but he showed from the very start that he was something special. Of course, as he told it, it was purely an accident he did so well against the Rangers.

"I got lucky and I scored two goals against Gump Worsley, who was minding the New York net," said Bobby.

Tommy Ivan, at the moment coach as well as manager of the Hawks, was so impressed with the boy's showing that he summoned Bobby's parents to St. Catharines. After four hours of hard bargaining, Bobby became the second youngest man ever to join an NHL team.

It wasn't long after the 1957 regular season opened, in the Hawks' seventh game, that Bobby scored his first NHL goal. Later, he tended to deprecate it, but at the moment he was quite proud, despite the goal being something of a fluke.

"It was against Boston in Chicago and Harry Lumley was the Bruins' goalie," said Hull. "Somebody rapped me a good one, and down I went—right on top of the puck. All I did was slide into the net with the puck underneath me."

For the first time he was able to raise his hockey stick in the traditional scoring salute he was to repeat more than 500 times in the next 13 seasons and more than 50 times in three of them, something no other man ever had done.

He was still a center, having been shifted back from left wing. His wingmen were Eric Nesterenko and Ron Murphy. He did well enough for boy or man, scoring 13 goals and 34 assists in his season. But he was passed over for the Calder Trophy as rookie of the year in favor of Toronto's Frank Mahovlich, a 20-goal scorer. As a center, he was a good wing.

"It was to be a couple of years before I learned about passing," he admitted later.

By that time he had been shifted again to left wing by Pilous, who had moved up from St. Catharines to coach the Hawks. Pilous reasoned that passing ability wasn't as important in a left wing. Besides, Hull's great left-handed shot made him a natural at the position. Pilous was right and Bobby proved it.

In his second season the boy with the shock of thick blonde hair was on his way to greatness. The Golden Jet had arrived. He proved it beyond doubt by leading the NHL in scoring with 39 goals and 42 assists for 81 points in his third year to become at the age of 21 the second youngest man ever to win a scoring title.

At that time, Hull was a "swinger," with a normal young man's appetite for raising cain. He was unsophisticated, like most Canadian youngsters who from the ages of 13 or 14 spent much of their time in hockey camps, schools, and games. This was to change, not that Bobby ever lacked the innate modesty and good sense that was to become even more marked as his fame increased. But with the passage of time he added complexity and balance to his natural intelligence, becoming an increasingly shrewd and reasonable man.

At 21, he liked more than his share of fun. Having a good time was all important. On a wild train ride from Boston to Montreal, Bobby and Ron Murphy discovered a case of railroad flares. They broke into the case and began lighting the flares, tossing them into their teammates' train roomettes.

After several hours of pandemonium and $600 worth of damage, Ivan called a team meeting. The players, including Hull and Murphy, silently filed into the car in which Ivan had set up his tribunal. The general manager calmly surveyed the group of young men.

"All right, who did it?" he finally demanded.

"I decided I'd better say something," Bobby recalled, "so I piped up, 'I did, sir.' Ivan just said, 'That's all I wanted to know,' and walked away."

Even then the more serious future was moving in on the carefree present. In the fall of 1959 Bobby met Joanne McKay, a slim ice-show skater from Los Angeles who was appearing at the Stadium. In February 1960 Bobby and Joanne were married. Ten years later they had four sons and a daughter.

Increasingly, during the following years Hull's thoughts turned to providing for this growing family. He began to cash in on his fame in hockey by widening his activities in other fields. His picture began to appear on advertisements for hockey equipment, sportswear, table hockey games, hair cream, and even automobiles and tractors.

He became the first hockey player to fully capitalize on his fame in the way athletes in other sports have done for many decades. The offers grew more lucrative after his 50-goal seasons and the most valuable player awards of 1964-65 and 1965-66. And his personal goals changed. Not that he no longer enjoyed playing hockey. But no longer an end in itself, it has become partly a means to an end. As he passed one milestone after another, he made that clear.

"I couldn't care less about getting 500 or 600 or any other number of goals," he said. "I never have been concerned with breaking anyone's records or catching up to anyone. I'm only concerned with using hockey to set me up in other things. I want to retire without having to go to work for anyone else. As soon as I can do that, I'll quit."

But no one can play a game as well as Hull plays hockey without having his heart in it. He also made that clear.

"Do I play like I enjoy it?" he once demanded. "Well, that's your answer. If I play well, I'm enjoying it. If I wasn't playing well it would be another matter. I don't think you can play hockey well without enjoying the game. But I do know that I don't want to play hockey for 20 years, that I can't play hockey for 20 years. It just isn't in me to do that."

Many reasons explain Bobby's reluctance to attempt matching the career longevity of players like Detroit's

Gordie Howe. Chief among them is concern about spending enough time with his growing family and the desire
to have his children grow up in the country, nearer to
nature than they can get in a big ctiy.

"One day Joanne called me to come to the window and
said, 'Come and look at Bobby sliding down the hill.' I
don't want to miss things like that," Hull explained. "You
have only one chance to see your children grow up and if
you miss it it's gone for good. I want my boys to grow up
in the country, like I did, and I want to watch them do it."

As soon as he began making good money, Bobby in-
vested in cattle ranching. His investments haven't always
worked out, but despite setbacks he is determined to make
this his career after his hockey days end. The interest in
cattle ranching started out when he was a boy.

"Some of our relatives owned ranches, so we spent a
lot of time on them when we were boys," he explained.
"When I was a boy I dreamed of owning a ranch. When-
ever we drove past one I always got a thrill out of seeing
the white-faced Herefords out in the fields. I'm no city
boy and never could be. As soon as the season is over I
want nothing but my farm."

Hull is no gentleman farmer. He pitches hay with the
help. "It's the best conditioner in the world," he main-
tains. When he reports for hockey training each fall he is
in better condition, if possible, than when the season ended
the previous spring. His love for the soil, for cattle, is so
deep that he would rather talk about the stock he owns
in Saskatchewan than about his hockey feats. His love for
animals is genuine.

"We went to the bullfights when we were in Spain a few
years ago," said Hull, "and I hated it. It was just a
slaughter. I cheered for the bull but I knew every time
one was brought in to the arena it was going to get
slaughtered and it bothered me."

His wife Joanne confirmed Bobby's feeling for animals.
"You can't believe," she said, "the number of times I've

practically driven into a ditch just to avoid hitting a frog.
We stop so that rabbits and squirrels can cross the road."

This is what makes Bobby not quite single-minded about
the pursuit that earns him more than $100,000 a year. And
it's part of what has made him such a determined negotiator
when it comes to agreeing to a contract with the Black
Hawk management. He is absolutely determined to provide for the future to such an extent that the things he
loves most will be available to him, that he won't ever
have to work for anyone else. That feeling was behind
his announced retirement prior to the 1968-69 season,
when he felt the Hawks weren't giving him as much as he
thought he was worth. He missed just one game, then
apparently got what he wanted and showed up for the second game of the season. Then he got more than even he
bargained for—from the crowd.

"I didn't even take a warm-up after I signed and got into uniform," he recalled. "But when I came up the stairs
onto the ice the crowd spotted me and realized for the first
time that I was back. The ovation I received made me
tingle. I was so embarrassed that I felt like crawling under
the bench and hiding from them, but I gotta admit I was
awfully proud."

That he always has been, and pride as much as anything else was behind his long disagreement with the Hawk
management the next year. Again he threatened retirement, charging the Hawks had failed to live up to the terms
of the contract he had signed in 1968. By the time the
argument was patched up, he had missed 12 games and
was to miss two more before he was fit to play. Whatever
the merits of either side in the disagreements, the basic
issue has been Hull's pride in his achievements and his
evaluation of himself as of equal value with the great
stars of any other sport, along with the determination to
extract full value for work received. Not that hockey has
become more work than fun, but there are many other
responsibilities connected with being a central figure in
the sport.

"Hockey itself isn't really becoming that laborious," said Hull. "It's the other responsibilities that make me anxious to get away from the game. They can really make you mentally tired."

How tired he didn't realize until one day his father's words jolted him to awareness.

"My dad worked harder than any man I ever knew," said Bobby. "But one day he said to me, 'Robert, you're going to kill yourself. You don't ever let yourself relax!' When he says something like that, it's enough to scare you."

The signs point in one direction. The likelihood is that Bobby will retire from hockey when he is 35. When he does, hockey will lose the greatest gate attraction in its history. With Hull, the Hawks have set attendance records in every NHL city. When six new teams entered the league for the 1967-68 seasons no team drew as well in their arenas as did the Hawks with their scoring machine, Bobby Hull. It isn't only the dynamic playing style that attracts fans; it is also the indefinable magnetism of Bobby Hull's personality, a quality vouchsafed seldom to an athlete and then only to those of the caliber of Babe Ruth and Red Grange.

Hull is a balanced compound of gentleness and toughness. His presence of mind and sense of the fitness of things are extraordinary for a man with his limited formal education and small town background. Unlike some athletes, he doesn't scorn fans, but almost revels in them.

"Every professional athlete owes a debt of gratitude to the fans and management, and pays an installment on it every time he plays," said Bobby. "He should never miss a payment."

The fans respond overwhelmingly to Hull. No athlete spends more time signing autographs or chatting with his admirers. Coach Reay and his teammates often have to force Bobby to leave after a game. At times, he has to be smuggled out of an arena through a seldom frequented exit.

In Canada the hero worship of Hull exceeds even that in Chicago. A Toronto lawyer tells the story of arriving at the airport at 5 a.m. one day to find the Black Hawks dozing in the waiting room, awaiting a return flight to Chicago.

"I was with a friend who had four boys, ranging from about 6 to 12 years old," related the lawyer. "One of the kids started up to Hull. His father said, 'Hey, you can't do that,' but quick as a flash, Hull was awake and, by God, there he was with a kid on each knee."

As gentle as Bobby is with children, he can be harsh if he has to be with obnoxious pests who often harass athletes. Bobby enjoys a beer now and then, and after a Chicago White Sox baseball game he had attended with friends, he stopped at a Michigan Avenue bar. A character came up to where Hull was sitting and started to insult him.

"Get lost, creep," Bobby snapped at him.

"You know something," said the pest, "you're a———."

Bobby reached across the table, grabbed the character's tie, twisted it, and slugged him. Then he slammed the man's head on the table. Dazed, the character crawled out of the bar.

"Later I find out he's a small-time hood and packs a gun," said Bobby. "I've never been back there since."

The point of that anecdote is that Hull can handle himself in any situation, pleasant or otherwise. He is probably the most accommodating and most pleasant public figure for a newspaperman to interview. He makes a point of being available.

"Like it or not, it's the truth that you could be the best hockey player in the world, but your acceptance and the acknowledgment of your ability would be limited so much that you would be totally frustrated if it were not for the sports writers satisfying the public's insatiable need to know," Bobby has advised fellow athletes.

Hull's awareness of the value of publicity may be conditioned by another ambition. He hopes someday to sit in the Canadian Parliament. It would not be a unique achievement for a hockey player, Red Kelly and Lionel Conacher, stars of the past, having been elected to Parliament. But that's still far in the future for Hull. First, he is more concerned with attaining financial independence by the time his hockey career ends. As he said:

"That's what everyone looks forward to, I'm sure. If you're not looking forward to financial security when you're in this game, you're not thinking straight. When I'm through playing hockey, I don't want to have to punch a time clock. I want to be able to do what I enjoy the most and to have security doing that. That's what everyone works for and invests for and that's what I'm doing with the farms."

The most exciting hockey player of his generation has a burning ambition that goes beyond scoring goals:

"I want to become the best breeder of polled Hereford cattle in the world."

16

Not One Alone

IT WAS like a game of "cat and mouse"—only this time the "mouse" pounced on the "cat." The "mouse" was Chico Maki, Black Hawk right wing, who skated right up to Montreal goalie Charlie Hodge and stole the puck from under his whiskers.

Maki's daring theft on the night of January 4, 1967, in a game with the Montreal Canadiens at the Stadium, led to the second of two goals by Bobby Hull. Both goals provided perfect illustrations of the help from linemates that even a player with Hull's talents needs, to score as often as he does.

With the Hawks trailing 2-1, Maki took a pass from center Phil Esposito at mid-ice and streaked across the blue line, firing a shot that goalie Hodge caught on the chest.

"He put it down," said Maki, "and faked a clearing pass, but held the puck with his stick while a Montreal defenseman moved to my right, from behind the net. Hodge was planning to pass off to the defenseman, but I chipped the puck away from his stick. Then I went around in back of the net, and when I saw Bobby coming I threw the puck out to him."

Hull, streaking in from left wing, picked up the puck and slapped it past Hodge from 15 feet out.

An earlier goal by Bobby also had been the result of close cooperation. Maki picked up the puck deep in the Hawk zone and fired it over to Esposito on the right boards. Hull was streaking up ice when Esposito hit him with a long, perfectly timed pass. That was all Hull, with his great ability to fake—"deke" as the hockey players term it—needed to get set up for a goal.

"I hollered to Phil and he gave me the puck," said Bobby. "I went up the middle between two Montreal defensemen. I dropped my shoulder, as if to go to the right, and when the defensemen parted I hit between them."

Bobby's deception then took care of goalie Hodge.

"He seemed to move to the left when I shot to the right," said Bobby. "I was going to the left of him and I was on stride that way, so he must have thought I was going to shoot in the same direction."

It is Bobby who most often provides the finishing touch on a goal, but he is the first to admit that without such skilled linemates as Maki and Esposito, and more recently Maki and Eric Nesterenko, he would not be so consistently a high scorer.

"The guys I've played with always have made things easy for me," said Bobby. "Bill Hay and Murray Balfour were good, and Phil Esposito and Chico Maki suited me even better. The day Phil, Chico, and I were first put together (in 1964) the team went on a 13-game winning streak. I know there have been a lot of great lines, but I think we made picture goals to match anyone."

Ronald (Chico) Maki, a Hawk regular since 1962-63, never has been a high scorer, reaching a peak of 17 goals in 1965-66, but getting goals has never been his main job. His greatest value has been in digging out the puck for Bobby and his outstanding defensive play both at right wing and center.

Ivan terms Maki, "A good, honest, hard-working hockey player whose records don't indicate how valuable he really is."

One record, however, does give a hint of Maki's value. When Hull scored 54 goals in 1965-66, Maki assisted on 16 of them, more than any other player, including Esposito, center of the line.

"It's a tremendous feeling to know I can take the puck and go up ice with only one thought in mind—to score—because Chico is going to be down there checking for me defensively," said Hull. "Without him, I would have to be more careful than I am about leaving opposing forwards an opening."

Maki, born in 1939, always has played a subordinate role in the line built around Hull. His job has been to provide defensive support and scoring opportunities for Bobby and even the third man, whether Esposito as in the past, or Nesterenko and Angotti as in 1969-70.

Reay rates Maki one of the finest forwards in the league and among its most aggressive players. Phil Esposito, while centering for Maki and Hull for three seasons, agreed.

"No one can compare with the hustle Chico has," said Esposito. "He amazes me every game with his constant checking. And, like Bobby, I could concentrate a lot more on offense because of it."

Reay and Ivan have consistently been aware of Maki's value to the Hawks. For the last couple of seasons it has been greater than ever as he and Nesterenko have been teamed up as penalty-killing forwards. In 1969-70 the pair set a record by holding opposing powerplays without a goal for 19 consecutive games. And the Hawks gave up just 32 powerplay goals in the entire season, less than any other team in the league.

Unfortunately, in retrospect, Ivan and Reay lost confidence in Phil Esposito after three seasons, particularly after his mediocre play in the 1966-67 Stanley Cup play-offs. In May 1967 they traded him to Boston along with right wing Ken Hodge and center Fred Stanfield in exchange for defenseman Gilles Marotte, center Pit Martin, and

goalie Jack Norris. Esposito's tremendous success since
then belongs more properly in a history of the Boston
Bruins. And Stanfield and Hodge haven't done too badly
either. Marotte and Norris were disappointments to the
Hawks; only Martin lived up to their expectations. It was
a trade that came to be thrown up to Ivan again and again
by the fans and press during the following two seasons as
the Hawks floundered and Boston began to soar with
Esposito, Hodge, and Stanfield playing superbly. For
Bobby Hull, the trading of Esposito, a close friend, was a
shock. He just couldn't understand why it was made.

"Phil, Chico, and I were hardly ever away from one
another off the ice," said Bobby. "And they knew how
to bring out the best in me. I need the puck a lot to be
effective, and they got it to me. We may have acted care-
less or looked bad in practice, but we always knew we
could do the job."

Ivan traded Esposito although the big (6 feet 1 inch,
195-pounds) center scored 23, 27, and 21 goals in consecutive seasons for the Hawks. He traded him partly
because of his disappointment in the big man's play in
Stanley Cup competition. Ironically, in 1969-70, Esposito
set a record for most goals scored in the play-offs with 13
as he led the Bruins to the Stanley Cup.

Perhaps Ivan's great mistake is that he mistook
Esposito's carefree, happy manner for lack of aggressiveness. Also, Esposito is a deceptive player, hard to size up
on the ice.

"Phil is so big and gangly that there is no place on the ice
that he can hide," remarked an NHL official. "A lot of
players can cover up their mistakes but Phil is too big and,
besides, he is always in the middle of things. So everyone
sees his errors."

Understandably, Esposito at first was hurt by the trade
to Boston. Later he realized he had benefited enormously:

"I came to realize it was the biggest break of my career.
Playing with Hull, you know he's the shooter. He's the best

in the league and you have to pass to him. Then you have to follow up by getting in position for the rebounds. With the Bruins you have more of an opportunity to shoot for yourself. But I learned a lot from Bobby, and we'll always be the best of friends."

Esposito's place as Hull's "feeder" was taken over at first by Martin. But this was a short-lived experiment, and Bobby usually has been teamed up with Maki and Nesterenko, with Lou Angotti spelling one or the other from time to time during the 1969-70 season.

By this time, with Bobby, 31, a subtle difference in his style had changed the role of his linemates slightly. More than ever, Bobby employs a pass to a teammate rather than taking the shot himself. Bill White, a defenseman whom the Hawks obtained in a trade from Los Angeles in February 1970, explained the advantage Bobby has in setting up his linemates:

"Hull comes at a defenseman so quick he's hard to judge. Not only you can't figure when he might shoot, but many times he doesn't shoot, he draws you in and lays off a perfect pass to a teammate. He makes greater passes than most people realize. He makes such great passes because defensemen have to concentrate on him. You can't take your eyes off him or leave him for a moment. So you naturally don't give the other players on his line the attention most players get and they're always loose."

It is a new kind of Bobby Hull and whoever may be his linemates of the future, they'll find, as Reay predicted, that they've got an increasingly subtle and more canny left wing than did their predecessors.

17

The Tormentors

BRYAN WATSON never took his eyes off Bobby Hull. As Hull moved in toward the goal, waiting for the centering pass, Watson tore after him. Hull had his back to Watson as the little Detroit Red Wing player raced in behind him and threw a cross-check, extending his stick vertically and slamming it into Bobby's back. The pain was excruciating, especially because Hull at the time was suffering from bursitis of the hip.

Bobby went down in a heap on the ice, writhing in pain, but when he rose to his knees, he swung his stick at Watson's head. He connected solidly and it was Watson's turn to go down on the ice, the blood gushing from his cut forehead.

"My stick came around and I clunked him," is the way Bobby put it. "I feel badly about it. It is not in my nature to do this. Sometimes I hate this game because of the way it changes a man."

Watson staggered off the ice, his ears ringing with the cheers of the Stadium crowd applauding what Hull had done to him. The period ended a few minutes later, and Hull entered the trainer's room where Watson was getting 18 stitches to close the wound on his forehead.

"I'm sorry," Hull said to Watson. "I meant to hit you, but I didn't mean to maim you."

"It's a long season," snarled Watson and it was a threat, not a statement of fact.

That incident, on November 19, 1966, is but the most memorable of a series of encounters Hull has had throughout his career with players assigned specifically to guard him. The job of "shadowing" Hull has been called the toughest task in hockey. It is a job that in recent years has gone to Claude Provost of Montreal, Ron Stewart of New York, Ed Westfall of Boston, Reggie Fleming with various teams, and, of course, Watson, who gained notoriety with the Detroit Red Wings in 1965-66 and 1966-67 and has bounced around since.

Unquestionably, it is Watson, of all the "shadows" whom Hull has had to contend with over the years, who has irritated him the most. Watson has never risen above the journeyman level as a player, but in his ability to gall Hull he has been a superstar. This is an art in itself, because Bobby is the most even-keeled of men. There is no doubt about his feeling for Watson, however. Hull has said:

"I don't like the look in his eyes. He has an air about him that irritates me. He's crazy. But primarily I don't like him as a hockey player and I don't like what he stands for. His tactics don't do anything for hockey. It's like bullfighting when there's a guy around the bull sticking those spears in it. If hockey were played by everyone like this nobody would come to the games."

These are strong words from Hull, who seldom complains about the flagrantly illegal tactics used against him. He is constantly subjected to interference, cross-checking, and boarding, but has come to accept the run-of-the mill violations of the rules that are not called penalties by the referees when directed against him. If anything, he is regarded as being too long-suffering.

"If Bobby hauled off once in a while and hit a few guys in the face they would start thinking twice about hounding him," said a teammate. "They would steer clear of him as they do of Mikita. They know if they try anything with Mikita, he'll go after them with the stick."

Coach Reay puts it more simply: "Bobby is just too nice."

Hull understands, even if he doesn't appreciate, that the shadows are dedicated to their duty, that they are committed to keep him from getting away clean shots at the net. What he resents are their tactics, especially those employed by Watson. As he explained:

"The thing that gets me most is when they stick so close to me that they don't even worry about getting the puck. I don't mind a guy going up and down with me. That's part of the game. But if he isn't trying to play any offense at all, he's not doing hockey any good—he's just hurting the game."

Montreal's Provost, a craggy-faced veteran right wing, irritates Bobby the least because he continues to play an offensive game at the same time that he is shadowing Hull. Strangely, Bobby almost has grown fond of Provost as his shadow and admires him as a player.

"Provost is all right," said Hull. "He guards me closely, like others do, but he plays his game, too. When the chance comes he goes on offense and gets the odd goal himself. He's the all-around hockey player!"

It takes an all-around player like Provost to do a clean, thorough job of shadowing Hull. The task can be thankless and frustrating, for just a momentary slipup may result in a goal by Hull. The shadow must keep the puck away from Bobby and vice versa. That is not easy. It takes a good skater to keep up with Hull and a great deal of strength to out-wrestle him for possession of the puck or to tie him up along the boards. Hockey is violent enough normally, but more than the average amount of brute strength is needed to contain Hull. He is tripped, shoved, poked, elbowed, speared, jostled and boarded far more than the average player. No subject can infuriate Reay more than the treatment Hull has received over the years, often under the eyes of referees. He declares:

"It's a crying disgrace what they do to Hull. He is constantly being hooked, but because he is so strong and good he refuses to go down and the referees don't call the penalties they should. I would guess that the referees would call a penalty nine times out of ten if Bobby would fall. I've suggested this to him but he's too proud to do it. If he can stay up he does."

Hull explained why he won't carry out Reay's suggestion and take a few "dives":

"When they trip me I keep going because I can do it. If I took more dives they'd get more penalties, but that's not my job or my way. Besides, I think the referees do a good job. Sure, they miss a lot of key penalties and the grabbing that goes on in front of the net, but those things are hard to see."

Reay is much more worked up than Bobby about the treatment accorded his great player not solely for Hull's sake but because he thinks it hurts hockey and is unfair to the fans. Said Reay:

"It's a shame that the most colorful player in the NHL has to be checked illegally. This is nothing new. It has been going on for a long time. It's done not only to Bobby. Other stars are getting the same treatment from players who can't keep up with them. All I ask is that Bobby be treated like everyone else. I know for sure that Maurice Richard and Boom Boom Geoffrion didn't have to put up with it when they were scoring 50 goals, and there's no reason Bobby should.

Hull, as befits the winner of the Lady Byng Trophy for sportsmanship in 1964-65, has been amazingly restrained in his reaction to shadows, although, as the Watson incident showed, he can be goaded to fury. He has admitted:

"Shadows get my goat. I'd like to be able to play like everyone else does. I know that there have been shadows for other players, but they didn't do it every game. I don't think there ever has been a guy they did it to as much as they do to me. Every game. The shadow business doesn't give you a chance to do what you'd like to do— get the puck and skate with it."

Hull, however, doesn't hold a personal grudge against

the shadows, with the exception of Watson, and that only because of the way he did the job while under the orders of Detroit coach Sid Abel. He says:

"These guys are only doing what their coaches tell them to do. The coaches are more responsible than the players. They give the orders because they're trying to get their teams into the play-offs to save their jobs. I don't think I would do it if I were coaching, but maybe I'm slightly prejudiced."

By thus placing the blame on the coaches Bobby more or less absolves Provost, Westfall, Stewart, and others who occasionally shadow him, but there is no forgiveness for Watson.

"Watson was always cross-checking me, running at me, high-sticking me," said Hull. "There was no need for the things he did. Sure, he was under orders to shadow me. But I can't believe that he was ordered to do the things he did."

From time to time the shadows have succeeded in curbing Hull. Boston coach Harry Sinden credited Westfall's work against Hull in the 1969-70 Stanley Cup semifinals between the Bruins and Hawks as being partly responsible for the four-game sweep over Chicago. Bobby went an entire game without a shot on goal and failed to score in the series.

"When we went into the series we knew that if we could stop Hull and Mikita we had an excellent chance of winning," said Sinden. "I think Westfall did a tremendous job on Hull. That was the key to the series, keeping him down."

Hull shrugged off the notion that Westfall had stopped him, faulting himself for his failure to score. Over the years, Bobby's record bears out his attitude that if he fails to score he mostly has himself to blame. Despite being shadowed in almost every game, Hull has averaged close to 50 goals a season for a long time.

Not only is the job of shadowing Hull thankless and punishing, but quite often it is fruitless as well.

18

The Defenders

PIERRE PILOTE waggled the puck for an instant on his stick behind the Black Hawk net, then began wheeling up ice. By the time he crossed the New York Ranger blue line he was in full motion, yet alert to the chance of completing a pass. He noted New York defenseman Harry Howell preparing to check Hawk wing Ron Murphy, sweeping in on the right. Pilote kept coming, moderating his pace.

"I wanted to wait until I had Howell in the right position," he explained. "I wanted him to commit himself either to me or Ronnie. When he came toward me, Murphy was clear and I passed to him."

The maneuver forced Ranger goalie Jacques Plante to move out to cut down the angle in the event Murphy took a shot. Instead, Murphy whipped the puck over to Eric Nesterenko, who was charging in behind him as the trailer. Plante was caught out of position and Nesterenko drove the puck into the net. That was the second Hawk goal in an otherwise forgotten game with the Rangers in 1964. As much as any one of Pilote's 400 assists in a dozen seasons with the Hawks it demonstrates the great value of the defenseman who three years running (1962-63, 1963-64, 1964-65) was awarded the Norris Trophy as the NHL's best at the position.

Pilote, whose rugged profile was taken by many to have

been the prototype for the Indian head on Hawk uniforms, was a rushing defenseman. He may have been the best of his type before the days of Bobby Orr. With Pilote on the ice, the Hawks really had four forwards. They also had a leader and recognized it, Pilote being team captain for several seasons, until he was traded to Toronto for forward Jim Pappin in May 1968. Until Boston's Bobby Orr came along to smash all offensive records for defensemen, Pilote held the NHL record for most points by a backliner—with 59, on 14 goals and 45 assists in 1964-65.

As good as he was on offense, particularly in bringing the puck out of the defensive zone, Pilote in his prime also excelled defensively. Although a small man at 5 feet 9 inches, he was a master of timing in delivering a body or hip check and was seldom caught out of position. He seemed to do everything right by instinct, although this was deceptive.

"He is one of the most natural players I've ever seen," said Ivan. "He anticipates plays almost before the opposition knows themselves what they're going to do. He is always a step ahead of the other guy."

Pilote's brains as much as his physical skills made him the outstanding defenseman in the league through the mid 1960's.

"His biggest trouble is being too intelligent," remarked Reay. "Sometimes he tries to outthink the other guy and, if the guy doesn't do the orthodox, Pierre is left standing there like a rank amateur. But the mistake usually isn't his, it's just that the other guy didn't do the right thing."

Pilote didn't outsmart himself too often. From the time the Hawks acquired him at the age of 23 by buying the Buffalo (N.Y.) franchise as a farm team in 1955, Pilote was their outstanding defenseman until he began to slow down. Year after year he was an All-Star team selection. But during his last two seasons with the Hawks, the fickle fans at the Stadium began to boo him for the slightest mistake—or what they thought was one. The harsh treatment finally "got to" Pilote and affected his play. He was almost relieved to be traded to Toronto.

A hockey wit perfectly described the situation: "The day Pilote is inducted into the Hockey Hall of Fame at Toronto a contingent of Black Hawk fans will be on hand —to boo lustily when his name is announced."

In Pilote's last three seasons with the Hawks he was teamed up with Doug Jarrett, a 6 foot one inch, 205-pound defenseman who provided the heavy hitting for the pair. In Coach Reay's tactical system, a rushing defenseman like Pilote is often teamed up with a bigger but still mobile defenseman like Jarrett, who can make a venture into the Hawk zone a painful experience for an opposing forward.

Before the advent of Jarrett, Pilote's partner on the back line for half a dozen seasons was Elmer (Moose) Vasko, (6 feet 3 inches and 220 pounds), one of the more formidable defensemen in the league. Vasko did a solid job for the Hawks for ten seasons, playing on the Stanley Cup team of 1960-61. When he slowed down four seasons later, Jarrett, then 20, got his job and Vasko faded out of the Hawk picture.

It was with Pilote and Jarrett in one defensive combination and with Pat (Whitey) Stapleton and Ed Van Impe in the other that the Hawks won the league championship in 1966-67. The aggressive, hard-hitting Van Impe was lost in the expansion draft the following summer, but Stapleton was to become almost a "new Pilote" for the Hawks.

Stapleton, a light-haired, chunky player (5 feet 8 inches and 175 pounds), born in 1940, plays much as Pilote did. He is a good skater, adept at bringing the puck up ice and having a good shot from the point, which makes him a natural choice for the powerplay unit. His 50 assists in 1968-69 set a record for defensemen, which was wiped out by Orr the following season.

Reay not only compared him with Pilote but eventually, at the start of the 1969-70 season, named him the succeeding team captain after a year without one. Said Reay:

"He's very much like Pilote in that he has good anticipation. A guy whose anticipation is working may be crossed up once in a while by the other guy and look bad, but it's a great thing to have going for him."

Stapleton's heady play and the deft way in which he uses his hands to bat down pucks and set up shots quickly are part of the flair that has endeared him to Hawk fans.

"They say he uses his hands well because he's built so close to the ground," joked Reay. Then, turning serious, he said:

"This is even more important on offense than on defense. Let us say we are up in their zone and we've got a guy in the slot and Pat is at the point. He gets a pass that's bouncing, or one that comes off the boards. He can knock it down with his hands and get a shot off quickly. Or he can keep it from getting by, which could mean trouble."

Many otherwise capable hockey players are unable to use their hands to the extent Stapleton does.

Said Reay:

"It's an indication of good reflexes. Some guys stand there with both hands on the stick. When the puck comes to them, they can't take their hands off the stick. Pat has got his hands loose on the stick and he is always ready to go after the puck. The greatest art is being able to get control of a bad pass. Maurice Richard scored a lot of extra goals because of that. He could pick up a puck with both his hands and feet."

Pilote, Stapleton, Jarrett, and Van Impe formed a well-balanced consistent defensive group for the Hawks in 1966-67, and there was little quality lost when the fifth man, Matt Ravlich, stepped in. Ravlich had been the regular the season before and it was a tribute to Van Impe's aggressiveness that he was able to take his job. It also showed the depth of the Hawks that they were able to use a man of Ravlich's quality as a spare.

The dark-skinned, handsome Ravlich, then 28, was the unfortunate victim of what seemed to the Hawks an attempt by the Detroit Red Wings to cripple them as a team for the play-offs. The incident happened in the final game of the regular season in the Stadium on March 29, 1967. Nothing was at stake for either team, the Hawks already having clinched first place and Detroit having been eliminated from contention for a play-off position. But the Wings came on the ice as if they were playing a Stanley Cup game, hitting hard and seemingly undeterred by penalties.

Ravlich got a chance to break through toward the Detroit net when he was hauled down by defenseman Bert Marshall. Ravlich slid into the boards and fractured both major bones in the lower part of his leg.

"I knew what had happened as soon as I tried to regain my balance," he said. "Mikita came skating over and I said, 'My leg is broken.' 'Nah,' Stan said, 'It's a pinched nerve. I had one just like it.' 'Like hell it is,' I told Stan. 'I know it's broken.' I don't know how many times I had gone into the boards that way without getting a scratch, but that time I just hit the wrong way."

A broken leg can end a hockey player's career. Often he is unable to regain his skating speed or stamina. Ravlich was determined not to let that happen to him. He spent six weeks in a hospital. He was on crutches for 4½ months after that. It was a year later before he again played for the Hawks. Although he played regularly in 1968-69, he never quite recovered his former skills with the Hawks. They left him unprotected in the player draft of 1969, and he was finally picked up by Detroit.

The injury to Ravlich was the the first of a series of mishaps that began to plague the Hawks in the midst of their joy over winning their first Prince of Wales Trophy. At the time, it seemed just a small cloud on otherwise beautiful skies.

19

Man With a Goal

IT IS NOT Billy Reay's style to thrust himself into the spotlight—the glare that outlines many men so sharply while coaching a team of professional athletes. He is a proud man, this coach of the Black Hawks, yet soft-spoken (although not unwilling to speak his mind). His words and thoughts, as well as leadership, have had much to do with shaping the Hawks into first-place teams in 1966-67 and again in 1969-70.

Reay got the Hawks to the top for the first time in their history in 1966-67 in his fourth year as their coach. He did it by instilling respect for himself in the players, by forming them into the proper combinations, by utilizing their talents fully—and by getting rid of those who in the past couldn't or wouldn't produce.

He has said:

"The only thing I like to stress to my players is that I make the decision. If I'm wrong, well and good. I won't blame them. That'll be my mistake. And I won't second guess myself by making some move I shouldn't make and then kick myself in the pants."

When Reay succeeded Rudy Pilous as Hawk coach in 1963, he found a team that had gotten out of hand and too many players who treated the training rules lightly. Reay could understand a man's desire for fun but couldn't condone it if it affected his ability to play hockey. He has said of himself:

"I'm a fellow that lives a pretty clean life, and I believe this is the easiest kind of coach to play for. If you get a fellow who starts coaching who has been a rough guy, a tough liver himself, he is harder on his players than a fellow like myself. He is always suspecting the players of doing what he did himself at their age.

"I feel I know the tricks, and I think the players know that they can't fool me. But I don't make a major issue of incidents, I only have to watch them skate to know exactly whether they're taking care of themselves or not."

If the players are breaking training rules, or if they're making mistakes on the ice that Reay feels can be corrected, he has his own way of handling them:

"It is very seldom that I blast a player in front of the whole team. It would have to be something that really got under my skin. I believe it is better to take the player aside—not right at the time, but the next day. Bring him into the office and have a talk with him. Try to draw out of him whether he realizes the mistakes he has made. If he doesn't realize this himself, then I'm in trouble. I've got to get to work and convince him that he's wrong. But in most cases the players know these mistakes and they're trying to rectify them all the time. If a player is doing nothing, he'll never make a mistake.

"A typical example is Pierre Pilote. A lot of people think Pilote made a lot of mistakes, but he had the puck so much that he was bound to make a mistake once in a while. This is what I mean. Some players never want to touch the puck, so that they'll never make a mistake. This is what we're trying to encourage in the boys all the time— don't be afraid to make a mistake; at least, you're trying to do something."

Reay's primary concern since he took over in 1963 has been to emphasize defensive hockey:

"I was very lucky to take a club that had such stars as

Mikita, Bobby Hull, Pilote, and Hall to start with. What I had to do here was to come up with the combinations where we had the defensive play in there as well as the offense."

Reay pointed out that a team's defense is dependent not only on the defensemen and the goalie, but also on the forwards:

"I like the goals. I like a lot of goals scored, but I also like good defensive hockey. I think a team's success is based on its defensive record. I think that realization of this gradually rubs off on the players. You stress these things and it takes a little while for it to have an effect. I feel that any hockey player has pride in his defensive record although he doesn't get the credit for it that he should have.

"Take players like Bill Hay, Eric Nesterenko, and Chico Maki, forwards who are terrific defensive players—tough hockey players to play against. They don't get the credit the goal scorers such as Bobby Hull and Mikita get. On the other hand, they're just as valuable.

As coach, Reay has a continuing struggle to convince goal-hungry forwards of his point of view. Often he has succeeded. He also has had the difficult task of convincing other players they should be satisfied with and could perform effectively in part-time roles:

"It is a very tough thing for a player to do, to sit on the bench for, say, 40 minutes then be thrown on the ice for a shift and be able to produce right away. I didn't feel I could do this as a player and I'm always on the lookout for players that can. I believe that we came up with probably one of the best I've ever seen at this in Lou Angotti. I can have Angotti sitting on the bench for any length of time, and then he'll get out there and be just full of hustle and bounce and spirit. This ability is a tremendous asset to a team."

These are but some of the considerations and points of view that enabled Reay, a small, stocky and dapperlydressed man, to reach in 1967 a new height in a career that started thirty years before as a player. He was good enough to play for eight seasons (1946-53) as a topflight center on several championship teams with the Montreal Canadiens. He said:

"I never dreamed as a youngster that I would ever coach the Chicago Black Hawks to their first league championship. This was a thrill for me that I just can't describe. It was a thrill because I knew exactly how much each player in our locker room had given to make this possible. We had wonderful spirit and willingness to achieve this goal. I give all the credit to the players."

It is never quite that simple. The players would agree that Reay deserved a great deal of credit for getting the best out of them. He is able to do this because he treats them with respect, something not every coach accords his players.

Like every coach, Reay has been down as well as up. In the light of later success, it is easier to look back with detachment, yet Reay admitted that the year 1960 was not the brightest of his life. He was fired as coach of the Toronto Maple Leafs in November 1959 after only a season and a half on the job. For the first time in his adult life he was out of hockey. Reay recalled:

"I stayed out a year partly because of disappointment— and, well, moves like this do affect your family. My wife and two children suffered probably more than I did. The Toronto management actually got me a job on a newspaper in Toronto selling advertising space, and I worked at that for a year. But I found that I walked the floor more being out of hockey than I ever did being in it. I don't know why. It's just in your blood. I've been in hockey, I guess, too many years to be out."

Hockey got in Reay's Canadian blood when he was a boy in Winnipeg, where he was born August 21, 1918, and it was firmly entrenched in his system by his early twenties, when he turned professional in the Detroit Red Wings farm system. Reversing the usual process, he became a coach even before he became a big league player.

"In Quebec City I was coach and manager when I was 23 years old. I guess the easiest part of it was that I led the club in scoring. When you're that young and you can produce yourself, they can't point a finger at you."

Reay led the Quebec City team to the Allen Cup, the senior championship in Canada and as a player intrigued the Canadiens. They made a deal for him with Detroit and for eight seasons he played center at Montreal, some of the time with Rocket Richard as a linemate. Reay's greatest day as a player came in a Stanley Cup game.

"One semifinal game in Boston I scored four goals, and I hit the post on another shot or I would have tied the record of five goals in a play-off game set by Rocket Richard. But the most gratifying year I had was when Boom Boom Geoffrion was a rookie on my line and scored 30 goals."

It is noteworthy that Reay played on lines with Richard and Geoffrion, two of the three men to score 50 goals in a season, and is coaching the third one, Bobby Hull.

Reay played on two Stanley Cup winners and one NHL championship team at Montreal before returning to coaching in the minor leagues after the 1952-53 season.

"They wanted me to play another year in Montreal, but I didn't feel that I was the right temperament not to play a regular shift. If I'd played another year it would have been killing penalties and spot work. I just wasn't built along the lines to do this."

What he *was* built to take was the responsibility of coaching, which he did in the minors for several years before getting the job of coach of the Toronto Maple Leafs in 1958. He viewed his dismissal in the middle of the following season as the "club's prerogative," but thought it unfair. He had been asked to rebuild the Maple Leafs but had not been given time enough to do the job.

"We were going through a period of trying to put youth on the club and sort of experimenting to see what young-

sters would mature. The next year we acquired some seasoned players—Allan Stanley, Johnny Bower—the kind of
guys that would be instrumental in the club improving.
But I didn't last that long."

Fortunately, he lasted long enough to make an impression on Hawk general manager Ivan. He and the late Jim
Norris, co-owner of the Hawks, hired Reay to coach in the
minors. After five years at Sault Ste. Marie and Buffalo,
Reay got the big job in Chicago in 1963.

He wasn't impressively successful at the beginning.
Every season he would spur the Hawks into hot stretches
in which they would take over the league lead. Then in-
evitably, lacking balance and bench strength, the team
would fold in the stretch. It became the common charge
the Hawks were not a team but a collection of selfish glory
seekers. Perhaps the loudest cry went up after Reay's first
season, 1963-64. Five Hawks—Hall, Pilote, Mikita,
Wharram, and Bobby Hull—were chosen first-string All-
Stars, and a sixth, Vasko was chosen to the second team.
Yet the Hawks finished second.

It took until the 1966-67 season for Reay to prove the
"snipers" wrong, something that must have pleased him
immensely. His major fault may be a tendency to deeply
resent criticism of his players coming from any other source
than himself. Sitting atop the league at the close of the
1966-67 season he could not possibly have been aware of
the sea of criticism and storm of troubles that lay ahead
before he would emerge again with a winner. As so often
happens, triumph was merely prelude to disaster. Yet for
a man like Reay the challenge is more than half the fun of
coaching. His ability to survive and surmount the chal-
lenges, almost to thrive on them, has made him the best
known and longest reigning coach in Hawk history.

20

Decline and Fall

IF A MOMENT could be pinpointed for the start of the Hawks' decline from the crest of hockey, it would be the instant Bobby Hull's puck struck Toronto goalie Terry Sawchuk in the left shoulder.

The Hawks and Toronto were battling in the fifth game of the Stanley Cup semifinals at the Stadium on April 15 1967. Each team had won two games and the score was tied 2-2 after one period, when ancient goalie Johnny Bower went over to Toronto coach Punch Imlach.

"I'm feeling shaky," Bower told Imlach. "My stomach's bothering me. Maybe you'd better take me out."

Imlach agreed. He didn't want to send in Sawchuk, who had been battered and bruised by the powerful Hawks in the first four games of the series, but there was no choice. It was obvious Bower was not fit to continue. Imlach sent in Sawchuk in the second period.

The confident Hawks, sensing a chance to take command of the series, greeted Sawchuk with a furious attack. Just two minutes after the period started Bobby Hull swung around at Sawchuk's left, just 15 feet away, and exploded a shot. The puck struck Sawchuk's shoulder and knocked him down and out.

As Sawchuk lay on the ice, Pierre Pilote skated by.

"How do you feel, Terry?" he asked. "You should have let it go, Terry. Might have been a goal."

Bob Haggert, Toronto trainer, shuffled across the ice to help the dazed goaltender. "Where'd you get it?"

"On my bad shoulder," replied Sawchuk, rising to his knees.

"Think you're all right?"

Sawchuk pulled himself to his feet, reached for his stick and snapped. "I stopped the damn shot, didn't I?"

He had done that, and he stopped 13 others in that period and 22 in the final period to shut off the most potent offense hockey had known up to that time. Toronto won the game 4-2 and then defeated the Hawks in the sixth game to win the series en route to a Stanley Cup.

"That's the greatest goaltending I've ever seen," admitted a chagrined Reay. "Nobody has ever played goal better than Sawchuk did in those two periods. He's the guy that beat us."

The Hawks' failure to add the Stanley Cup to their Prince of Wales Trophy was a tremendous shock. Many experts had hailed the 1966-67 squad as the greatest hockey team in history. Yet it had failed in the first round of the Stanley Cup series against a lightly regarded Toronto team, which had finished fourth during the regular season.

The disaster may have warped the judgments of Ivan and Reay. Almost immediately after the Toronto series was concluded Ivan vowed changes would be coming even in advance of the draft to stock the six expansion teams that were to join the league in 1967-68.

"Too many guys didn't do a job for us in the play-offs," said Ivan. "Our biggest failure was at center. We're going to have to trade to get an established center and we need help on defense."

Shortly thereafter, in May, came the celebrated trade that sent Phil Esposito, Fred Stanfield, and Ken Hodge to Boston in exchange for Pit Martin, Gilles Marotte, and goalie Jack Norris. Admittedly, the trade was made in part to prepare for the draft, in which the Hawks were sure to be hurt.

"I know it's for the good of hockey," said Ivan, "but that doesn't make it easy. You work for years to build up a team, finally get the players you need to achieve depth, then lose it all at once. I'm all for expansion, but it still hurts."

The Hawks were deeply hurt by the draft. They could protect only one of their top two goalies, so they chose to keep Denis DeJordy and let St. Louis take Glenn Hall. It was to prove a mistake, but an understandable one. De-Jordy was much younger and Hall had threatened several times to retire and might at any moment. Besides, Hall no longer wanted to play in Chicago because the fans were down on him.

The Hawks also lost Angotti, Van Impe, Hay, Vasko, and several lesser players. At one blow the depth Ivan had worked for years to provide had disappeared. Seven men were gone from the championship team. Another, Ravlich had a broken leg and could not be counted on for the 1968-69 season.

"We're going to have to go all out just to make the play-offs this year," said Reay, when camp opened in September 1967. "We just haven't got the depth we had last season, and Glenn Hall was worth six to ten points to us. But I've got confidence in DeJordy. He has all it takes to be a top NHL goaltender."

Reay's reliance on and confidence in DeJordy were understandable. DeJordy had played for him when he was coaching at Buffalo and had been an extremely steady performer while sharing the job with Hall in 1966-67. There was no reason to suspect that he would fail. In any event, a tall, slender young schoolteacher named Dave Dryden was also on hand.

The Scooter Line of Mikita, Mohns, and Wharram was still intact, and Reay saw Pit Martin fitting in nicely between Bobby Hull and Chico Maki. The chief problem up front seemed to be to find a center between right wing Eric Nesterenko and left wing Dennis Hull. Here came a real problem, Reay reluctantly settling upon Jerry Goyer, 31, a veteran minor leaguer, and a small, converted defenseman, Paul Terbenche, to share the job. Rookie forwards Wayne Maki and Bill Orban also were available.

The defense seemed solid. Jarrett, Pilote, and Stapleton were back and Marotte, only 22, a powerfully built man (5 feet 9 inches and 195 pounds) appeared to be a future All-Star, tough and aggressive. Tom Reid, 21, a big, handsome ex-collegian seemed ready to fill in when needed.

When the season started, however, nobody seemed ready for anything. The Hawks lost their first six games, then slowly came alive as DeJordy improved in goal and the Scooter Line powered a resurgence. The Hawks lost just four of their next 31 games, winning 18 and tying nine, to reach the halfway point of the season with a creditable record.

During that span of 31 games, Mikita, Wharram, and Mohns piled in 47 goals. Mikita got 21 of them, on his way to a 40-goal season and his fourth scoring title with 87 points. In one stretch of 16 games, Mikita scored 13 goals and 18 assists, for an average of almost two points a game.

It was this surge that rescued what otherwise would have been a disastrous season. The Hawks, slumping badly in the second half, easily could have dropped out of a play-off spot. As it was, they barely beat out Toronto and Detroit to finish in fourth place. In the second half, The Scooters fell off, injuries hampering Wharram and Mohns. The aging Pilote slowed down badly and Marotte failed to play up to expectations. Goyer and Terbenche were just adequate, and Wayne Maki was a disappointment. Orban, and another young forward, Bob Schmautz, filled in respectably. Martin, the little center on whom Ivan had counted heavily, never could get started as Bobby Hull's "feeder"—although the big left wing did score 44 goals. An ankle injury suffered in December bothered Martin the rest of the season, and he ended up with only 16 goals.

Ivan was under heavy fire by the press for the trade with Boston. Phil Esposito, Hodge, and Stanfield were producing for the Bruins. Ivan retorted:

"I wish people would give Martin a chance. Never try to judge the value of a trade when it is first completed. It may take a year or two to actually judge whether or not it is a worthwhile trade. The Bruins received some badly needed punch and we received a top defenseman, a great center, and a potentially good goalie."

Time was to prove Ivan's point in respect to Martin, who did turn out to be a superb center. On the other hand, Marotte, although he played fairly well in his first season with the Hawks, failed to develop as expected. He had a tendency to get caught in the corners, and to get rattled and give away the puck at awkward moments.

A couple of seasons later, just before Marotte was traded away, the burly defenseman made a charge up the length of the ice with the puck and blasted a shot at close range on the goalie.

"You know," said Ivan, his eyes following Marotte, "that's the first time in the years since we got him that Marotte has done that. And we got him just for that purpose. We thought, the way he can skate, that he'd be doing that for us regularly. He never has."

He never did and turned out to be one of the greater disappointments of Ivan's career as a trader. Goalie Norris proved to be just a journeyman.

It was to Reay's credit that he managed to drag this patched-up crew across the finish line in fourth place. And that he was able to get it past the New York Rangers in a bitterly fought quarterfinal round of the Stanley Cup playoffs, before going down before powerful Montreal in five games in the semifinals.

In retrospect, the 1967-68 season was notable chiefly for

the continuing development of Dennis Hull, Bobby's younger brother by five years, having been born November 19, 1944. It is Dennis Hull's burden to be so closely related to hockey's most famous goal-scorer. It caused him to be brought up to the Hawks before he was ready in 1964-65. He had to be sent to the St. Louis farm club for most of the following season to improve his skating.

He played a solid role in the championship drive of 1966-67, scoring 25 goals. Despite his patent awkwardness on the ice, the fans seemed to take to him at first. They seemed to enjoy the unmistakable resemblance to Bobby—the swooping figure setting up the puck at the blue line, the slap shot whose velocity left the goal almost paralyzed as it crashed past him into the net. Then, in the early part of the 1967-68 season, Dennis couldn't find himself. It was clear he missed the canny Bill Hay, who as center the previous season had set him up for so many goals. The fans turned on him. Though it was unfair for the fans to do this to a young player, Dennis let it get him down, admitting they had cause for their complaints. The barrage of abuse from the galleries became so vicious that it shocked even Pilote, who had become pretty much a target for hecklers himself in his final year with the team. Pilote was hardened to the abuse, but he spoke up in defense of Dennis.

"When they boo you every time you step on the ice, how can a player get loose?" Pilote demanded. "Everyone can see that Dennis presses. He's thinking about every move. I'll tell you something. You can't think too much in this game about what you have to do; you have to react instinctively."

Pilote's concern for Dennis was not just out of sympathy, but an appreciation of his potential and desire:

"If he was a different kind of guy, I wouldn't care about the booing and all that. Some young players need a few boos to shake them up a little, and the guy who buys a ticket has the right to boo me or anybody else. But Dennis tries. All the time. That makes a difference.

"Dennis has a great future. He wants to be as great as his brother. We know that this isn't likely to happen, but the important thing is that the kid wants to be great. And he's going to make it."

Dennis agreed with Pilote's insight of his aspirations, declaring:

"When you love hockey and you want to be good, and when your brother is already there and you know what it's like when a player does make good, that gives you added incentive. Bobby is the greatest hockey player in the world, and it's a thrill just to be his brother. If I'm just half as good as he is I'll be a good player. There's no shame in not being as good as Bobby—a lot of other guys could say the same thing, yet they're good players."

The comparisons with Bobby are unfair to Dennis. As Eric Nesterenko said, "Dennis is a good major league hockey player in his own right. That's the way he should be measured."

From the first, Dennis was measured on his own merits by the Hawk organization, including Coach Reay.

"Dennis is a nugget in the rough," said Reay, when he first got a look at the younger Hull in 1964. "He has to improve his skating and acquire a little polish and finesse. He's rugged enough (5 feet 11 inches and 195 pounds) and has a National League shot. And no one works harder than this boy. He has the desire to play hockey."

The desire may yet make Dennis one of hockey's finest players, not on a level perhaps with Bobby or Stan Mikita, but on the next rung.

"He's capable of scoring 30 to 35 goals a season," said Reay. "There's no telling how far he can go with his willingness to work and his shot."

Dennis seemed to pick up after his slow start in 1967-68. He was playing chiefly on a checking line, but managed to end up the season with 18 goals. And the following year he was going to live up to Reay's forecast.

At the conclusion of the Stanley Cup play against Montreal, which ended with a 4-3 defeat in overtime in the fifth game, Ivan and Reay could look back at the 1967-68 season with muted satisfaction. Said Reay:

"I think we've done a good job just to get into the play-offs. Look at Toronto; they came into the season with 11 National League forwards, yet they didn't get into the play-offs. We lost seven men from last year's championship team and yet we made it. We have been able to develop some young players, like Marotte, Schmautz and Dennis Hull, who should be able to help us even more next year."

Ivan expressed satisfaction with the accomplishment and looked ahead to the summer trading. "We have the same old problem. We could use a big center, maybe two. We could also use another right wing."

Encouraged by the development of Marotte and Reid and the apparent recovery of Ravlich, who rejoined the team during the play-offs for the first time since his serious injury the year before, Ivan and Reay decided Pilote, now 36, was expendable. They traded him to Toronto for Jim Pappin, a 6-foot one-inch, 190 pound right wing who had quarrelled with Coach Imlach.

The trade turned out well for the Hawks, for Pappin was to prove of considerable help the next two seasons, while Pilote lasted just a year at Toronto, then retired.

When the 1968-69 season opened it seemed the Hawks were on the rise. The devastation left by expansion had been repaired. True, DeJordy hadn't had as good a season being the No. 1 goalie as he had when sharing the job with Glenn Hall in 1966-67. But his goals against average of 2.80 in 1967-68 was respectable, and Dryden had done a fair job of filling in.

On defense, the Hawks seemed solid—with Stapleton, Jarrett, Ravlich and Marotte; and just before the season opened they picked up an experienced veteran, Howie

Young to be the fifth man. Young had been with them in
the 1963-64 season and had established a reputation as the
wild man of hockey, then had been dropped for violating
training rules. Now, after a stretch with Detroit, he was
back, although reformed.

Reay took Martin off the Bobby Hull line and placed
him between Pappin and Dennis Hull. Chico Maki moved
from right wing to center on Bobby's line, with Eric Nesterenko moving into his spot. The Scooters, of course, remained intact. Orban and Schmautz were available as
extra forwards.

But trouble started even before the season opened. A
few days before the first game, Bobby Hull shocked the
hockey world by announcing his retirement. Bobby had
been unable to reach agreement with management on the
terms of his contract. Reportedly, he was seeking $100,-
000 a year and a long-term pact. At the same time, Mikita
was holding out, reportedly asking for $75,000. Mikita
signed his contract on the evening of the opener and got
into uniform just before the face-off. Bobby missed the
game, but ended his "retirement" a couple of days later in
time for the second game.

The Hawks, with Pappin leading the way, got off to a
fast start, winning their first four games. Pappin scored
six goals in the first three games, including the first hat
trick of his career against Minnesota in a 10-4 rout. By
Christmas he already had 19 goals, six more than he had
scored the entire previous season at Toronto.

By that time the Hawks already were staggering. Goalie
DeJordy seemingly had come apart. His confidence shattered, he was shaky, and shots from the blue line were going past him for goals. On November 11, 1968, just a
month into the season, the Hawks sent DeJordy to their
Dallas farm club to recover his confidence. Dryden and
Norris were to share the job until he returned. Dryden
and Norris, however, didn't prove equal to the job. The
team continued to flounder, and when DeJordy returned

after a few weeks at Dallas he didn't seem greatly improved. Reay spoke up for his beleaguered goalie.

"It's not DeJordy's fault," insisted Reay. "The guys in front of him are letting him down, and I don't mean just the defensemen. It's up to the forwards to get back and help out on defense. They're not doing it. We've got a general letdown on defense, and if we can't get improvement we're going to have a hard time making the play-offs."

Christmas Day 1968 presented a new problem. In a game against Toronto at the Stadium, Bobby Hull was struck on the jaw by Maple Leaf defenseman Mike Pelyk's elbow. X-rays disclosed a hairline fracture and it was predicted Hull would be sidelined several weeks. Bobby proved the prediction wrong. He missed just one game. With his fractured jaw wired and wearing a helmet fitted with a face guard, he returned to the ice. If the Hawks continued to stumble it wasn't because Hull had lost his scoring touch. Despite the injury, hampered as he was with the face guard blocking his view of the puck at his feet, he scored 10 goals during the 18 games and six weeks that followed, bringing his season total to 32. When the wire came out of his jaw and the helmet off his head, he cut loose with 19 goals in the next 14 games, crashing past the 50-goal mark for the fourth time in his career. On March 20, 1969, in Boston, he scored his 54th and 55th goals of the season to set a new record. Ten days later, in the final game of the season, he scored No. 58.

Joy in the individual achievement was marred by sorrow for the team's failure despite the offensive power of the Hawks. They had settled into sixth place, finishing on the bottom of the division and missing the play-offs for the first time in 11 seasons. It was possibly the best last-place team in any sport in history, winding up with a winning record (34-33-9) but that didn't lessen the sting.

As the season wound to its dreary close, highlighted only by Hull's drive toward a new goal-scoring record, the fans turned on Coach Reay. The chants of "Goodbye,

Billy, we hate to see you go," became louder and more per-
sistent with every game. On one occasion, Reay was almost physically assaulted as he walked through the crowd.
Ivan also came under attack. The trade with Boston was
flung in his face at every turn. The critics were given
plenty of ammunition by the great season Phil Esposito
had with the Bruins, with 126 points on 49 goals and 77
assists. To round out the case, Hodge had scored 45 goals
and Stanfield 25. That added up to 119 goals scored by
the three men the Hawks had traded away, and now *they*
were in last place.

The Black Hawk management did not take the usual
way of a sports organization out of such a predicament:
fire the coach or dismiss the manager, or both. William
Wirtz, the elder son of Arthur M. Wirtz, who had taken
over presidency of the team since the death of Norris,
refused to panic.

"Good hockey coaches are hard to come by and Billy
Reay is one of the best," said Wirtz. "If there has been a
failure, it has been the failure of the entire organization,
not of one man or two. We are not going to put the blame
on Billy or on Tommy Ivan. We will assess the situation
and see what can be done to improve the club for next
season."

Armed with such loyal support, Ivan and Reay sat down
to assess the lessons of the immediate past and plan for the
future. For the first time, Reay admitted the team's primary failure had been in goal:

"There was no use talking about it earlier, but it was
the bad goal that was beating us. They were getting by De-
Jordy time after time. I can think of half a dozen games
we lost because of cheap goals.

"Sure, we weren't as defensive-minded as I'd like a team
to be. But bad goalkeeping contributed to that. Before
we knew it, we'd be behind 2-0 and then we had no choice
other than to open up to try to get back in the game and
that led to more goals."

Reay admitted to other problems. Defenseman Marotte, in his second year with the Hawks, had shown no improvement. Another defenseman, Mike McMahon, obtained together with center Andre Boudrias in exchange for Reid and Orban in a late-season trade with Minnesota, also proved inadequate. Ravlich couldn't regain his past form. Among the defensemen, only Stapleton had been outstanding and Jarrett more than adequate.

Up front, time was catching up with the Scooter Line wings Mohns and Wharram, both in their late thirties. Near season's end, Reay returned Mohns to defense, where he had spent the first 11 years of his career. The move foreshadowed the building of a new line around Mikita, who had a brilliant 1968-69 season, with 30 goals and 67 assists for 97 points to tie his career high.

Among the few positive aspects of the season was the rise of Martin to the level predicted for him by Ivan and Reay. The little (5 feet 7 inches, 165 pounds) center scored 23 goals and 38 assists while setting up his wings, Pappin and Dennis Hull each to 30-goal seasons. It was quite a turnabout from the previous season, when Martin had been hampered with an ankle injury. But Reay at the time cautioned critics not to downgrade Martin too quickly.

"For gosh sakes, give the kid a chance," said Reay. "He has got a bad ankle, and if you take away his skating ability he's bound to be in trouble. The poor kid's just out of luck this season. He's going to be a fine hockey player and he'll prove it one of these days."

Martin did prove it in the face of the Hawks' tailspin of 1968-69, and he was to prove it even more conclusively the next season. Perhaps even more important, his fine play in the year of disaster enabled him to speak out freely during the summer of 1969.

"The problem in Chicago is total lack of direction," said Martin, in an interview in the *Toronto Star*. "There is no leadership at all coming from the owners, general manager, or the coach. And when they aren't concerned the players aren't concerned either."

He added that only five players wore "their uniforms with pride."

William (Billy) Wirtz, instead of reacting adversely to Martin's temerity in speaking out so bluntly, applauded warmly and added, "Inconsistency and lack of dedication and motivation are the real reasons for the team's lacklustre showing." He thanked rather than spanked Martin for speaking out.

Martin, a French-Canadian born in 1943, was christened Hubert but got his nickname of Pit from a cartoon character in a French-language newspaper. He was just 20 when he first came up to the NHL with Detroit in 1963-64. He quickly earned a reputation for skating speed and hustle. He scored 20 goals for Boston in the season before being traded to the Hawks, including four goals one night at the Stadium. The ankle injury was not the only thing that bothered him in his first season in Chicago.

"I think the main thing that bothered me at first was that with the Hawks I'm expected to come back deep into our zone on defense. What I'd do with Detroit and Boston was to do deep forechecking and as the center I' be the last man down the ice on defense and take a point. Here I'm expected to do the forechecking as before, but then go deep in our zone on defense. It was hard to do at first, but it started working out for me. I began to get a lot of chances to bust down center ice when I got the puck behind our blue line. I think it's a better system."

In his second year with the Hawks, Martin clearly mastered the tactics advocated by Reay, gained confidence, and did so well that he could speak out on what he felt to be the shortcomings of the team. His words played a part in the regeneration of the Hawks.

Far more important, however, was a move Ivan made. In the summer NHL draft in June 1969, the Hawks claimed

Tony Esposito, Phil's brother, who had played 13 games in goal for the Montreal Canadiens late in the 1968-69 season.

For $25,000 Ivan acquired one of the great bargains of hockey history and set the stage of the regeneration of the Hawks.

Ivan and Reay had seen Esposito play several games for the Canadiens while their regular goaltenders, Rogatien Vachon and Gump Worsley were sidelined with injuries. In 13 games, Esposito, in the NHL for the first time, had shut out the opposition twice and registered a fair 2.73 goals-against average.

"I was impressed with the way he handled himself," said Ivan. "We thought he would be a fine back-up goalie for DeJordy and would take some of the pressure off Denis."

And Reay commented:

"What impressed me the most about Tony was his alertness. He was exceptionally alert even for a goaltender. He was constantly on top of every play. He didn't let up for a moment. You could see right away he didn't let his mind wander. We made up our minds that if he was ever available we'd try to get him. We had no way of knowing how good he actually was but we were willing to take a chance; especially, since goaltending was our weakness."

It was a weakness that $25,000 abolished. And the check for $25,000 that the Hawks turned over to Montreal restored Ivan's tarnished reputation as an evaluator of talent. He had made the biggest coup since he acquired Glenn Hall from Detroit a dozen years before.

For Tony Esposito was Mr. Goalie all over again.

21

Ashes to Gold Dust

ONLY A movie script writer with a morbid imagination could have dreamed up a less auspicious beginning for the Hawks' success story of 1969-70 than what actually took place. One blow followed another and there seemed little reason to expect much from a team that—in any event— had been relegated to fifth or sixth place in a national poll of hockey writers.

The most serious misfortune took place shortly after the opening of fall camp. Kenny Wharram, the veteran little right wing, suffered a heart attack on September 17 and for a time was in critical condition. Fortunately, he made a fine recovery, but it was clear that his hockey career had ended.

While Wharram lay in the hospital, Bobby Hull wasn't in camp at all. He had signed a four-year contract after his holdout of the season before but now charged the Hawks had failed to honor some promises made at the same time.

"I have no desire at all to leave Chicago," Hull told a newspaper reporter, "but I'm tired of all this trouble every year. If the Hawks don't want to deal with me, maybe they ought to trade me."

General Manager Ivan, contending Hull was under contract, waited for Bobby to call him. It was going to be a long wait.

There was also an undercurrent of unease at camp among the veterans. The memory of Martin's criticism of the management, coach, and players was still fresh. And Martin hadn't limited himself to generalities, but had made a pretty clean sweep of the team in his remarks, focusing particularly on the privileges he thought were accorded Mikita and Bobby Hull:

"There's a star conflict. The Hawks have one big star and one fairly big star, and the club seems to be set up to keep those two happy. The rest of us don't matter much. Players do as they please. Several players have only one ambition—to score goals, no matter whether the opposition scores more while they're on the ice. To sum up, there's a total lack of team spirit. Some of our players don't react after a victory. In fact, they're unhappy if they haven't scored. On the other hand, even after a defeat, they're quite happy if they've scored a goal or two."

Clearly, Martin had included almost everyone in his blanket criticism, but whatever his teammates thought, Coach Reay wasn't disturbed.

"I'm glad to hear that Pit was so angry over the way things went last season," said Reay. "He wasn't the only one. I was pretty upset myself and intend to do something about it this season."

Reay and Ivan did do something, setting up new guidelines for the players that placed everyone on an equal footing, from rookie to big star.

More important in the final analysis were the additions of personnel made by Ivan. Not only had he acquired Tony Esposito during the summer but had brought back little Lou Angotti, the spirit of the 1966-67 championship team, and another small center, Howie Menard.

Yet an even more significant step actually had had its beginning five years before. In February 1964 Ivan had made an agreement to supply players to the Los Angeles Blades, then a minor league team. In return, the Hawks were accorded the privilege of selecting several players from time to time from among those either playing for the Blades or to whom they had the professional rights. Exercising this privilege, on August 16, 1967, shortly before the Blades made way for the NHL Kings, Ivan acquired two students at the University of Denver, Keith Magnuson and Cliff Koroll. A year later, he claimed Gerry Pinder, a collegian who was playing on the Canadian National team.

Koroll, a 6-foot, 196-pound right wing, and Jim Wiste, a 5 foot 10, 185-pound center, also from Denver University, had played the previous season for the Hawks' Dallas farm club. They had done well and the scouts were particularly high on Wiste. Magnuson, a 6-foot, 185-pound defenseman, was a completely unknown quantity to Reay. As for Pinder, a 5 foot 8, 165-pound right wing, the Hawks did not add him until late in the training camp period.

To Reay's surprise and delight—and of necessity—all four youngsters showed enough promise to stick with the team. It was a gamble to go with so many rookies—Esposito and another defenseman, Ray McKay, also falling into this classification—but Ivan and Reay had decided the Hawks had no choice other than to rebuild.

Magnuson, just 22, a baby-faced redhead, won a regular job from the start. Wiste started out as left wing on the Mikita line. Pinder and Koroll for a time were shuffled off and on the bench, filling in where needed as Reay tried to rearrange his forces. The veterans Gilles Marotte and Doug Mohns alternated between left wing and defense. The Martin line, with Jim Pappin and Dennis Hull, was still intact and Reay patched up the third line—lacking Bobby Hull—around Chico Maki and Eric Nesterenko, with whoever appeared best suited at the moment, from among Lou Angotti, Howie Menard, Pinder, and Koroll.

Reay was impressed with Esposito during the exhibition games, but refused to commit himself as to whether Tony or DeJordy would be the No. 1 goaltender. He promised:

"They'll both get plenty of work. Goaltending is too tough a job these days for just one man. I may go a little longer with a goalie who is hot, but against certain teams, in certain cities, I'll use the man I think best for that game."

Esposito got first call, playing the opening game against the Blues at St. Louis on October 11. It was a disaster for the Hawks. They lost 7-2, and the only consolation was a pair of goals by rookie Pinder. The next game, the home opener, Reay switched to DeJordy, who played well. Still the Hawks lost 2-1 to Oakland, the team that had beaten them five times in six games the previous season and so dumped them into sixth. The skid continued, the Hawks losing their first five games before gaining a 1-1 tie in New York on the sixth attempt, largely on DeJordy's fine game in goal. Reay wouldn't admit discouragement although the fans were chanting, "Goodbye, Billy, it's nice to see you go." He declared:

"We didn't expect it to be easy. We've got six rookies out there and it's going to take them some time before they find themselves. It may take 30 or 35 games before we play the kind of hockey I believe we are capable of playing. But I'm not discouraged. With a break or two, we could have won two or three of our games. You don't get discouraged as long as you see everybody working out there."

The turning point came on October 25 at Montreal—of all places. In front of Esposito's superb goaltending, the Hawks—regarded as a pushover for the Canadiens—rose up to surprise them 5-0. No one then could suspect the significance of that first shutout for Esposito, but it was unmistakable that the team was beginning to find itself.

Not that the problems had ended. The veteran Mohns came up with a sciatic condition and went into the hospital, necessitating the return of Marotte to defense. Wiste proved a disappointment despite his fine showing in camp, and Reay began to rely increasingly on Koroll and Pinder. And Bobby Hull still was missing.

Yet the victory at Montreal apparently had revealed something to the Hawks—that they could win. They were so delighted that they shook off a succeeding defeat in Los Angeles, then won six games in a row, added a pair of ties and won two more before losing 5-4 to Detroit on November 29. They had run up a 10-game unbeaten string and, although just a step ahead of sixth-place Toronto, had a winning 10-7-3 record. Not only that; Bobby Hull finally had reached agreement with the management and was back on the ice.

The break had come on Friday, November 14, after the Hawks had played 12 games of the season and had a four-game winning streak underway. At an elaborate press conference in a Chicago hotel, Ivan and Hull disclosed they had reached agreement—but it was obvious the management had won the battle of wills.

Ivan made it clear in a statement that Bobby would have to subordinate his individual style of play to what the management considered was best for the team as a whole:

"We decided early in training camp to insert as many rookies as the club could stand and rebuild completely," Ivan said. "Understandably, we must be patient because of their inexperience. But our main concern is to get a maximum team effort, with aggressive as well as defensive play. After all, hockey is a team game. We do not detract from Hull's great ability as a hockey player or discount some of his spectacular efforts or contributions to the team in the past. But we learned last season that individual records do not win championships."

Hull chafed a bit at first under the new order, the emphasis on defensive and disciplined play. He got back on the ice for the Hawks' 15th game of the season, but he couldn't really get into topflight condition easily, although he started out averaging a goal every other game.

"There's no way I'll ever get in shape the way things are going," he grumbled. "I'm just not the kind of player who can go up and down his wing like he's on a string, playing 15, 16 minutes a game. That's just not my style."

His displeasure was just momentary, however. In a more relaxed moment, he admitted he had been impressed by the Hawks' new flair and style when he had watched them on TV during his absence, but that he had also been disturbed.

"I was at home watching the club play and I didn't get the gist of it until I got back," said Hull. "It frightened me at first because I was afraid I wouldn't get untracked in time. But from adversity comes good. It took me until Christmas to become a hockey player again, but I watched the kids and I marveled."

He well might have marveled for while he was absent the Hawks had become a "team" in the full sense of the word and had found themselves a superb goalkeeper in Esposito, who was gaining confidence with every game. No wonder. During the ten-game unbeaten string, Esposito worked every minute and gave up just ten goals, one per game. Two of the games were shutouts, one of them 1-0 over Montreal at Chicago, and in four others he gave up just a single goal.

The turnabout was complete. The team that had given up the most goals in the Eastern Division the season before suddenly had become the most difficult team in the entire league to score on, and continued to be so, right to the end of the campaign.

Reay gave full credit to Esposito and denied indignantly, almost vehemently, that the Hawks had changed their philosophy of play—or, at least, that he as a coach was doing anything differently:

"I'm firm about my convictions. I don't change them easily. I have the same ideas about how hockey should be played as I did a year ago. And we are not playing at all differently. You just don't always achieve what you plan.

"Hockey is different, in a sense, from other team sports. In most sports offense dictates the moves. But not in hockey; all your offensive plays depend on the moves of the defensive team. And the flow of the game makes you improvise. But, essentially, if you can keep the goals-against down, if your defense is sound, you're going to control the game. Your wingmen have to check as well as your defensemen.

"You always want your men to play positional hockey, not to the exclusion of offense but to the extent they are helping out the goalie. I've always stressed that—last year or any other year. The main difference now is Esposito, making the big saves game after game. If we're behind 1-0 he comes up with the big save and keeps the score from being 2-0, which is all the difference in the world. You can keep playing a tight-checking game, you don't have to open up. You can wait for the break.

"This is the difference. Last year, before we knew it, we'd be down 2-0 and then we had no choice; we had to open up to try to get back into the game and that led to more goals—but we started out the games the same way. Because Tony has kept us in the games, this year we've been able to stay with our plan. People talk about our improved defense and I'll admit we were blessed when young Magnuson came along and showed he was inter-ested strictly in keeping the other team from scoring. But the key has been Esposito's ability to come up with the big save. I can't recall in my six seasons here when we've gotten better goalkeeping over a long stretch."

There were other factors, too, in the Hawks' resurgence, among them the return of Bobby Hull and the play of the rookies. And despite succeeding injuries to key men such as forward Jim Pappin, Koroll, and Eric Nesterenko, the Hawks kept moving on, now chasing the four teams ahead of them, particularly fourth-place Detroit.

Reay, as enchanted as he was with Esposito, found room to praise Mikita, who had scored 20 goals by mid-season, and Stapleton, the superb rushing defenseman who also was keying the Hawks' offense.

"If any hockey player could be said to have played a

perfect game, Stan and Pat could be said to have played several of them," said Reay. "You can't say too much about the way they've been playing."

In one of the major readjustments of the season, Reay had placed Dennis Hull on left wing with Mikita, who with Koroll on right wing found himself flanked by two strong though unpolished players.

"The kids will make a few mistakes," said Mikita, "but they're working hard, digging all the time. You just have to be patient and appreciate that they are trying their best. When we get used to each other, goals and points will start taking care of themselves."

Making matters even more difficult for Mikita was the pain of a back ailment, stemming from an injury suffered late in the previous season. The little center had to wear a corset, yet overcame the discomfort to play as well as ever. For a stretch of 20 games at mid-season he averaged two points a game and climbed into third place in the scoring race behind Boston's Bobby Orr and Tony Esposito. Said an appreciative Reay:

"Mikita's having his greatest season. We've been getting by on goaltending and hard work, and Mikita has been showing the way in the hard work department. He has been a tremendous inspiration to the younger guys on the team."

Bobby Hull also provided inspiration. He scored four goals in his first six games and Magnuson, who was playing with him for the first time, was awed.

"You can't appreciate him until you've played with him," said Magnuson. "I wasn't around here last year, but the guys who were say Bobby never skated his position and came back to help on defense like he has this year. It's really nice, you know, to throw that puck up to Bobby on the left wing—and then watch it disappear."

Bobby kept making the puck disappear at a progressively faster rate, and with Esposito continuing his impressive goaltending the Hawks finally got off the .500 mark for good with a 7-0 victory over Detroit on January 7 at the Stadium. It was a critical victory because it kept the Hawks a point ahead of sixth-place Toronto and within eight points of fourth-place Detroit.

The Hawks were 15-15-5 going into that game. From that point on they were 30-7-4 through the rest of the season, losing just seven of their final 41 games.

As this tremendous drive began and the Hawks continued to win without visibly gaining on fourth-place Detroit, also going strong, Reay began to worry. He was convinced the Hawks had to beat out Detroit for a play-off spot. The three teams on top of the division, New York, Montreal, and Boston, seemed out of reach.

"Detroit and Toronto are the teams we've got to beat out," said Reay. "Sure, we're going good now but you always worry there might be a letdown after a hot streak. When a team has gone as well as we have for such an extended period, it's only natural to hit a bit of a drought, to level off."

He didn't dream the Hawks wouldn't hit their "drought" until the semifinals of the Stanley Cup play-offs. They roared through January and early February and yet on the evening of February 7, before a game against Philadelphia at the Stadium, still remained three points behind Detroit. They had won ten, tied one, and lost just two of 13 games, yet were still in fifth place.

The game against Philadelphia, a 4-4 tie, brought disaster. Pat Stapleton injured his left knee so seriously that he was out the rest of the season, and in May had to undergo surgery. Early in the second period of that game, with the Hawks leading Philadelphia 3-2, flyer forward Jimmy Johnson broke in on goalie Esposito. Tony managed to get a pad on the puck but it got away from him and appeared headed into the net. Defenseman Stapleton flung himself full-length on the ice and knocked the puck into the corner. But as Stapleton skidded across the ice his left knee smashed against the goal post. He suffered ligament and muscle damage. Although Reay was tremendously downcast by the mishap, he wouldn't go along with most observers, who felt the injury to Stapleton was a fatal blow to the Hawks' chances of making the play-offs. (Stapleton was the key man in the defense and a major factor on offense.) Said Reay:

"The other fellows will just have to take up the slack. Sometimes a thing like this just makes a team work all that much harder. Everybody tries to make up for the man who is lost. But there's no doubt we'll miss Stapleton. He can bring the puck out of our end better than any of our defensemen, and he has had some tremendous games on defense this season."

The next game, the following night, tried Reay's patience and fortitude even more. The Hawks and Montreal were tied 2-2 midway in the third period in the Stadium, when Bobby Rousseau of the Canadiens broke across the blue line. Hawk defenseman Marotte tried to block Rousseau's slapshot from 55 feet out, and the puck glanced off Gilles' shoulder to deflect into the net past Esposito. The Canadiens won 3-2, and Reay was furious.

"If we wanted our defensemen to play goal we'd put them in the net," said Reay. "We've had too many of that kind of plays lately. We're not taking out the man."

It was evident to Reay and Ivan that something had to be done to strengthen the Hawks' defense, in particular to make up for the loss of Stapleton. Rookie Paul Shmyr, who had been called up from Dallas, played well enough, but it was clearly too much of a gamble to risk all on an untried youngster.

On February 20 the Hawks completed a six-player trade with the Los Angeles Kings, getting veteran defenseman Bill White, goalie Gerry Desjardins, and Bryan Campbell, a young center. In exchange, the Kings received DeJordy, Marotte and a minor league player, Jim Stanfield. Desjardins had established a fine reputation as a goalie at Los Angeles and, at 25, was five years younger than DeJordy.

But White, 31, 6 feet 2 and 190 pounds, was the key player for the Hawks. He could carry the puck and, more important, was proficient in taking out the opposing forwards without drawing penalties.

Commenting on White, Reay said:

"He's not spectacular, but he does a solid, workmanlike job. He doesn't make too many mistakes. He's not going to dazzle anyone, but he's just the steady, dependable sort of defenseman we need. He was good enough to make the All-Star team in the West last season, and we've been after him for a year."

White was paired with Mohns, and Jarrett teamed up with Magnuson as the Hawks set their defense for the rest of the season. Shmyr filled in as the fifth man. Almost on command, the Hawks moved into fourth place the weekend following White's arrival—with victories over New York and Boston at the Stadium on successive days.

White's debut, against the Rangers on Saturday night, February 21, was truly a night to remember, not only because of the Hawks' 4-2 victory but because Bobby Hull reached the 500th goal of his career. Hull put in No. 500 midway in the second period and seven minutes later made it No. 501 (his 29th of the season), with White getting an assist. Hull thus became the third man in hockey history, behind Gordie Howe and Rocket Richard, to score 500 goals during a career.

While Hull was gratified by the achievement and the ovation he received from the Stadium crowd, he disclaimed any desire to set his sights on Howe's record. "I'm not even thinking about that," he laughed. "That would take a long time to do and Howe is still getting them."

But he was struck by another thought, and made a prediction, based on the mad rush in tandem with Detroit.

"You know, the way we're going now we could wind up on top, 1-2, with Detroit," said Bobby. "We could be fighting for a play-off spot and wind up in first or second place."

Reay refused to entertain the notion of finishing in first place, and even less of aiming for it. The sudden discovery that the Hawks, in their furious drive to pass Detroit had climbed to within two points of third-place Montreal, eight of second-place New York, and nine of first-place Boston, didn't alter Reay's viewpoint. He snapped:

"I'm not thinking about first place at all. And I don't want my players to think about it. We're going to have a tough enough time just making the play-offs. This is the most difficult part of the schedule ahead of us, with a six-game road trip, and later on, our last six games are against the clubs in our division. We'll be playing head-to-head and we'll have to do a lot better than we've done."

When Reay spoke, the Hawks were embarking on the six-game road trip, the longest jaunt of his seven seasons as coach. It was a severe test, and later on was regarded as the most critical period of the season. It proved a smashing success. The Hawks started with a 3-2 victory at Philadelphia on February 26, lost two days later 3-0 at Boston, but then won the remaining four games—at New York, Los Angeles, Oakland, and Philadelphia. In the process, they moved into third place, just three points behind second-place New York and six behind Boston.

Not even a 3-3 tie with Boston at the Stadium on March 11 could stem the growing conviction that the Hawks—despite Reay's disclaimers—were indeed in the battle for first. Just four days later the Hawks passed New York to move to within three points of Boston. The Bruins had 87 points to the Hawks 84, each team having nine games left to play. If the Hawks could win at Toronto on Wednesday, March 18, the game at Boston the following night would be a battle for first.

It worked out that way, the Hawks easily defeating Toronto 7-4 and thus moving to within a point of the Bruins, who now were ahead by just 87-86. But for the moment, the Bruins stemmed the tide, winning 3-1 over the Hawks on Eddie Johnston's superb goaltending and two goals by Johnny Bucyk and another by Derek Sanderson, to take Thursday night's game.

"We haven't seen the last of them," predicted Johnston, who had held off two powerplay rushes by the Hawks in the first five minutes of the game. "The way Esposito's playing goal for them and with the scoring punch they've got, they'll be in it right to the end."

Reay took the defeat well.

"I'd be a lot more discouraged if we'd given up after their third goal, when we were down 3-0," he said later that night. "But we kept right on working and even got the goal by Dennis Hull. As long as they don't give up on themselves they'll be in this all the way."

It was clear at this point that "in this" meant the battle for first, although Reay continued to maintain he was thinking only of making the play-off spot. But a 5-4 victory at Pittsburgh while Boston was losing to Minnesota the following Saturday reduced the Bruins' lead to a single point again. It also set up an unprecedented situation, with Detroit just two points behind Boston, and New York and Montreal tied for fourth, just four points out of first. The wildest race for first place in NHL history was underway with five teams having a chance at the Prince of Wales Trophy and each having seven games left to play.

"It's unbelievable," exclaimed Reay. "Five teams and each of them can finish either first or entirely out of the play-offs. The pressure is really on, but this is the way I like it. I wouldn't have it any other way."

He didn't get an alternative. On Sunday, March 22, Esposito tied the league record for shutouts as the Hawks defeated St. Louis 1-0 on a goal by Doug Mohns in the third period. It was Esposito's 13th shutout of the season, matching the record set by Toronto's Harry Lumley 16 years before. The victory kept the Hawks in step with Boston, which defeated Minnesota to remain a point ahead, 91-90.

And when the Bruins moved three points ahead by defeating the Rangers 3-1 at New York, the Hawks responded to the challenge the next night at Detroit.

"This was the turning point," said Reay later, and the game of March 26, a Thursday, at Detroit was a magnificent hinge of fortune. Both goalies, Roy Edwards of Detroit and Esposito were in top form. Esposito's save on Frank Mahovlich in the first period left even Reay stunned. Edwards played almost as well, making fine saves on Doug Mohns and Bobby Hull, and the teams battled through two scoreless periods.

Deep into the third period came the break. Pit Martin, the little center, who with linemates Pappin and Pinder had been carrying the Hawks offensively for weeks, took a pass from Koroll and streaked down the right side all alone. He fired once, Edwards making the save, but then losing the puck. Martin was in on the rebound and fired a backhand shot high into the air and over Edwards to produce the final score of 1-0. It was Esposito's 14th shutout, and Lumley's record, as well as the Red Wings', had fallen.

Both the Hawks and Bruins tied their next games to remain even until Sunday, March 29. While the Bruins were tied by Detroit, the Hawks defeated Toronto 4-0 to give Esposito his 15th shutout and to pick up a point that tied them with Boston for first place.

It was an incredible situation. With three games left, the Hawks and Boston each had 95 points. Montreal was five points behind in third place, a point ahead of fourth-place Detroit, which was a point ahead of fifth-place New York. Seven points separated the five teams. Four of the teams—Boston, Detroit, Montreal, or the Hawks—could finish first, while Detroit, Montreal, and New York still could miss the play-offs. The Hawks had an edge in that even if they finished in a tie on points, they had enough victories to be awarded first on the basis of having more than the other team.

"It's just like every year," remarked Reay, calmly surveying the prospects for the final week ahead. "Montreal is going to take a hand in this thing right to the end."

The Canadiens were—but not a hand they would have dealt themselves. They started out well enough, defeating Boston Wednesday night, not that it did the Hawks any good, as they lost to Detroit to remain in the tie for first place.

Now came the final weekend, the Hawks facing a home-and-home series starting at Montreal with the Canadiens. Boston had a similar series against last place Toronto. The odds had to favor Boston—when had Montreal ever lost two important games back-to-back?

But Saturday night, April 4, while the Bruins defeated Toronto, the Hawks swept past the Canadiens 4-1, with Dennis Hull scoring the winning goal, one of the biggest of his career. It was an astounding feat to win so important a game on Canadien ice, and Montreal forward Bobby Rousseau felt impelled to offer an explanation.

"Remember when they finished in sixth place last year and a man named Dissension played left wing for them," said Rousseau. "I noticed tonight when Dennis Hull got his 100th goal he skated and gave Billy Reay the puck to keep for him. You always give the puck to the trainer in a case like that. That must mean there is more togetherness between Reay and his players than anyone can imagine."

It was a flash of insight on Rousseau's part. Togetherness had carried the Hawks to the top and had kept them there until the final day of the season, when they beat the Canadiens 10-2 at the Stadium and put away the title with their 45th victory.

"It's hard to pick one man out for praise more than another," said Reay as the Hawks celebrated. "It has been a total contribution—from everybody."

It was, of course, but there was no doubt the greatest role had been that of Tony Zero.

22

Tony Zero the Roamer

THESE days Tony Esposito is a hero as the sensation of hockey in the nets for the Black Hawks, but there was a time when he was more often than not a scapegoat for his brother Phil, who is 14 months older.

Phil told the story, which happened when the brothers were in their mid-teens and living at home in Sault Ste. Marie, Ontario:

"I was a devil as a youngster. As a kid I was always playing practical jokes on somebody. I always believed in having a good time and I still do. There are three kids in our family. Besides Tony and me there is sister Terry, who is younger.

"I really got in trouble with my dad one time when I was about 16. I was supposed to be baby-sitting with the younger kids, but I took my dad's car, took Tony and put Terry, who was just a year old, in the back seat. We drove around quite a while and I lost track of the time.

"I can still remember coming home from the joy ride and noticing my dad's truck had pulled up while we were gone. I can tell you, I was scared. I panicked and sent in Tony first with the baby and waited outside to see what would happen before I went in. Dad gave Tony a smack and I can still remember him yelling, "Where's the other guy?"

Tony has long since forgiven if not forgotten taking that

first blow for Phil. He and Phil are still very close, even if one plays for the Hawks and the other for the Bruins, bitter rivals for NHL dominance. And Phil is still the practical joker, big and easy-going, while Tony is smaller and more intense, although sizeable enough at 5 feet 11 inches and 185 pounds.

They were born and reared in Sault Ste. Marie, the sons of Patrick and Frances Esposito. Phil was born February 20, 1942, and Tony followed on April 23, 1944. Actually, both boys are Anthony's, that being Phil's middle name. The family home in those days was in the heart of an old, mixed neighborhood with many nationalities and languages. Like most Canadian youngsters, the Espositos played their first hockey in the streets, progressing to neighborhood rinks as they grew older. They even shot pucks in the basement when no other place was available.

Their mother, Frances (a dark-haired woman whose looks Phil has inherited while Tony resembles his big, solidly-built father more) had a difficult time getting them to come home for dinner. It took Dad's shrill, piercing whistle to get them to moving on the double.

"They were always out there, every minute," said Dad Esposito. "It was always Phil shooting and Tony playing goalie. That's all they ever did. They'd have a few spats as brothers always do but they'd always make up right away. They were both good boys although Phil would play a few pranks once in a while."

Phil did do that, once setting the house afire accidentally while sneaking a cigaret in the basement.

At the age of 16, Phil left home for the Black Hawks' farm team at St. Catharines to begin his ascent to the big league and eventual stardom. Hockey was everything to him, and he quit school without his parents' knowledge. It wasn't until the school term was over that Pat and Frances found out. They pleaded with him to return to school, but Phil had no taste for studies and it was to no avail.

It was quite otherwise with Tony, who was able to combine hockey with his school work and even to participate in other sports. He was an all-city halfback on the football team at a Catholic boys' high school in St. Catharines.

Hockey didn't come first for Tony, but it came right after getting an education. Not that he was an instant success as a goalie while playing minor hockey. In fact, he quit at one time because of the abuse he was taking from his teammates after every defeat. Said he:

"I always felt bad when I'd let a winning goal get into the net. At that time I began to brood over the way the guys were talking to me and looking at me every time we got beat. We were all kids, but everybody wanted to win and nobody more than me. I felt it was my fault when I let a goal get by me and I knew the other fellows had the same feeling. They were blaming me and I thought they might be right."

After sitting out a season, Tony returned with a new attitude.

"I decided that I would have to take the responsibility for any goals scored on me. Regardless of how the guys play in front of me, I'm the last one that can stop the puck. If it gets by me, it's my fault. Of course, if the guys are playing a good defensive-type game it makes my job a lot easier.

With the new viewpoint, Tony resumed goaltending. He was good enough to get a chance to play for the Sault Greyhounds, a junior A team in the Northern Ontario Hockey Association and turned in a spectacular season. His goals-against average in the high-scoring league was 2.62, and that earned him a hockey scholarship to Michigan Tech University, the school that also produced Lou Angotti, the little Hawk center. Tony continued to put schooling first and earned a degree in business administration.

He played hockey at Michigan Tech for four years, earning All-American honors the last three. Among the teams he played against was Denver University, whose roster included three other future Hawks, forwards Cliff Koroll and Jim Wiste and defenseman Keith Magnuson.

"He did quite a job against us," recalled Koroll. "He shut us out twice, we beat him once, and the other game ended in a tie. But you could see then he was no ordinary college goaltender."

Upon graduation from Michigan Tech in 1967, Tony turned professional. The Canadiens had the rights to him, and they sent him to the Vancouver Canucks of the Western Hockey League. Tony played in 62 games and had four shutouts although his goals-against average was an unremarkable 3.20. The next season, 1968-69, the Canadiens called him up and he filled in while Worsley was injured and when Vachon went into a slump. He played briefly for the Canadiens' Houston farm team.

It was with Montreal that Tony faced Phil on the ice for the first time since their boyhood, playing goal in two games against Boston. The first time Tony shut out both Phil and the Bruins. Phil gained revenge the next time, scoring twice on Tony for the only two Boston goals in a 2-2 tie.

Naturally, the confrontation between the brothers attracted a lot of attention. Both Phil and Tony faced a barrage of questions about how it felt to be competing against each other.

"We're still very close and I love him like a brother," said Phil, "but he's a professional and I'm a professional. My job is to put the puck past him and he's out there to stop me. Blood is thicker than water but this is ice."

Back home in Sault Ste. Marie Mom and Dad carefully steered a neutral course. They were both pleased—almost astonished—to see both their sons in the National Hockey League.

"They were very good hockey players as boys," said Dad Esposito, "very good, indeed. I never dreamed they'd be that good. I really never thought they'd make it in the NHL. I thought Phil was pretty good with his stick and Tony a smooth skater, even better than Phil. But I didn't see anything in them as boys that stood out. They've gone far beyond anything I dreamed they could do, and I'm just pulling for both of them. When it comes to pulling for either of them against the other I can't be anything but neutral."

When the season ended and the Canadiens management assessed its personnel, the decision was made that Tony was expendable. He had played well enough, but Vachon was just as young and more experienced. And Worsley, while an old warhorse, had proved his value many times over. The Canadiens had won first place and the Stanley Cup two years in a row with them in goal, and there was no reason to think they couldn't do it again. They left Tony unprotected in the draft and the Hawks snapped him up.

Montreal's decision was one of those that swings the fortunes of a franchise. It was the making of the Hawks, while the Canadiens found out too late the extent of their blunder. Vachon played well, but Worsley got into a tiff with management and was shipped off before the season ended. The Hawks rose to first place while the Canadiens dropped to fifth, missing the play-offs for the first time in 22 years.

At first, the Hawks didn't quite realize the extent of their good fortune. Reay stated repeatedly before the 1969-70 season started that DeJordy and Esposito would share the job of goalie. And he figured Denis had the edge for the No. 1 job because of his experience. But neither man was too impressive at the start, the Hawks losing their first five games, then gaining a 1-1 tie at New York.

"I was beginning to wonder if I hadn't overrated Tony," said Reay. "I was beginning to think maybe we'd made a mistake. Then came the game at Montreal. That's the one that convinced me we had an exceptional goalkeeper."

When the Hawks took the ice the night of October 25,

1969, it looked like they would be in for a horrible beating. They hadn't won a game, the lineup was loaded with rookies and the champion Canadiens were on home ice. It figured to be no contest. It proved that way, too, except in reverse. Although the Canadiens flew down the ice, battering Tony with shots, they couldn't get the puck past him. When the game was over, the Hawks had a surprising 5-0 victory and a goaltender who had just taken his first step on the way to a record.

Coach Reay had played a hunch in starting Esposito against Montreal.

"I thought DeJordy played a tremendous game in the 1-1 tie in New York," he explained. "But I decided to go with Tony in Montreal in the hopes that he'd be fired up against the team that let him go, and it worked. I can't remember winning that decisively too often in Montreal."

With Esposito taking over the goaltending job more and more from DeJordy, the Hawks turned around to run up a ten-game unbeaten string. Tony began piling up the shutouts, with three in November, three in December and three more in January for a total of 10 in his first 36 games worked.

By mid-January his work earned the mid-season Vezina Trophy for the Hawks. With Esposito doing most of the work, the pair had given up just 87 goals in 38 games, one less than New York's goalies, headed by Eddie Giacomin.

New York Ranger Coach Emile Francis regarded Esposito as a flash in the pan. "He couldn't even carry Giacomin's stick," snorted Francis.

Tony's reply was brief. "Let Giacomin carry his own stick. I'll use the one I've got."

Francis' pique was understandable. Giacomin for several years has been the hardest working and one of the most highly regarded goalies in the game. His style is more orthodox than Esposito's, which has been called no style at all. Actually it is a combination of several styles, with a strong dash of free-lancing thrown in. Tony explained:

"As a kid I watched Glenn Hall a lot on TV, and also Johnny Bower of Toronto. I tried to pick up something from each one. Hall's a reflex goalie, and they call me the "unorthodox goalie" maybe because, like Hall, I depend a lot on reflexes. From Bower I've picked up the way he uses his stick. I try to poke check with it and I guess I use it more than most guys. I like to use the stick a lot and I'm not too proud to accept a little help from the goal posts, although they bounce off it against you about as much as they bounce for you."

Tony doesn't hug the goal posts, however, as do most goalies. He'll move off to the side a little, figuring he'll be better balanced to slide across the crease if the direction of attack suddenly changes. In short, he prefers to roam, and that includes coming out of the net much more daringly than most goalies. He comes out freely, often "wandering," as Reay complains, to cut down the angles even more sharply and to gamble on sweeping the puck away from an onrushing opposition forward.

Reay shudders at Esposito's forays. "I've asked Tony to stay in his net," said Reay, "but occasionally he seems to think he's a forward and comes out almost to the blue line."

And Tony's answer:

"I guess Billy's right, but it works for me. I know it makes more sense to stay in the crease, but once in a while you have to take your chances when the puck is loose in front and an opposing player is the nearest man to it. You've got to gamble a little. I never go for the puck unless I think I've got a better than equal chance of beating the other guy to it. I've been lucky most of the time."

Despite occasional tremors of apprehension when Tony takes a flier, Reay is rather pleased with his goalie's free-wheeling and confident reliance on his superior reflexes.

"He reminds me a lot of Glenn Hall. When he's behind that face mask and yelling you'd swear it was Glenn. And he has a lot of Hall's moves, the same quick reflexes. Also, he's like a third defenseman out there. He's in on every play. I've never seen a more alert goalkeeper. He'll never be beaten because he's asleep."

Esposito carries his stick in his left hand and catches the puck with his right hand. When he's crouching, his pads are touching, but his lower legs are bent outward so he can move in either direction freely. His position also keeps the puck from going through his pads, although occasionally he separates them to give the shooter a target, then snaps them shut, a feat requiring great timing. He has a way of dropping to his knees and spreading the pads out to either side on certain kinds of shots, mostly from the point. Sometimes he dips with his right leg when making a stop, but seldom touches the ice with his left knee unless he flops—which he does quite a bit.

One observer compares Esposito's style of playing goal with that of a shortstop in baseball. It's an apt comparison. Esposito has great range and his skating skill, even on the awkward goalie skates, is an asset that can't be discounted.

His steadiness under fire is remarkable. He gives the appearance of a man totally without nerves. It isn't quite accurate. Before the start of a game he betrays his nervousness by rocking slightly while the National Anthem is played. He admitted:

"I get nervous like anyone else, but during a game I haven't got time to think about it. You get keyed up, and if you're concentrating on what's going on, you're not aware of it. I try to stay calm as a game approaches, but in a way I'm glad I'm not. You have to be a little tense to function at your peak."

After a game, Esposito seems totally drained, but—unlike some goalies—is never on edge. And, true to the resolution he made years ago, he never blames anyone else for a goal scored against him.

After a disappointing game in 1969-70, in which Tony allowed a "cheap" goal, a Toronto sportswriter remarked: "That goalkeeper gives it to you straight every time—he doesn't alibi, does he? He's as calm as if he had had a shutout."

Brother Phil noted that Tony always has had an even disposition.

"Even as a kid, he never did get too nervous," said Phil. "He'd get excited once in a while, but mostly he was a pretty cool customer. Now, it's pretty hard to shake him up."

Tony proved that, as the pressure built up during the 1969-70 season. By early January the Hawks were starting to move, although still in fifth place, only Toronto behind them. A 7-0 rout of Detroit at the Stadium on January 7 put them over the .500 mark to stay (16-15-5) and they began their long and eventually successful pursuit of fourth-place Detroit.

Tony came up with back-to-back shutouts of Pittsburgh and Boston on January 14 and 17. The latter game was played in Boston and the Hawks won it 1-0 on a disputed goal by Gerry Pinder, the Bruins claiming the puck hadn't crossed the goal line. It was a defeat bitterly recalled later by Boston, which considered it had been officiated out of first place when the Hawks finished ahead at season's end.

The turning point of the game came in a confrontation between the Esposito brothers. Bobby Orr hit Phil with a lead pass as he was moving in on Tony. Phil ragged the puck, moved across the goal mouth, feinted Tony out of position and flicked the shot toward the open net. He didn't get enough wood on the puck and sliced it off the post. It bounced away to be swept into a corner by defenseman Pat Stapleton.

"You lucky so-and-so," Phil hissed at Tony.

Luck had little to do, however, with Tony's sweep toward the NHL record for shutouts in a season, set at 13 by Harry Lumley of Toronto in 1953-54. It was skill, with Tony playing as spectacularly as any goalie ever played. The night he tied Lumley's record with a fine effort against St. Louis at the Stadium with a 1-0 victory was a perfect example. In order to preserve the shutout, he had to stop canny veteran Phil Goyette from a few feet out, stop him again on a tip-in attempt in the third period, and smother a breakaway with just a couple of minutes left to play.

He accepted congratulations for his achievement calmly and modestly.

"A shutout is really a team award," said Tony. "All the guys worked so hard for me. They have all year. I appreciate it so. That's why I have 13 shutouts—their work. The other guys played so well that I kept thinking 'don't ease up . . . you don't want to let them down.' "

He never did let them down. Just four days later, in Detroit, he played an even better game, shutting out the Red Wings 1-0 in the game that Reay later regarded as the turning point of the season. A stop on Detroit's Frank Mahovlich in the first period left Reay stunned. Esposito was out of the cage, to his right, when Mahovlich came in on a virtually undefended net. As Mahovlich got off the shot, Esposito appeared out of nowhere to turn it aside.

"I've never seen a shot in my life that I figured was as sure a goal and then had it saved as the stop Esposito made on Mahovlich," said Reay. "I've never seen a better save in my life."

That save was just one of 35 Esposito made as the Hawks went on to win on a third-period goal by Pit Martin, and Esposito passed Lumley's record with his 14th shutout of the season.

Two days later, on Saturday, March 28, he held the Maple Leafs to one goal in a 1-1 tie at Toronto. The next day, in Chicago, he shut them out 4-0 to round out a new NHL record for shutouts in a season at 15. More important, the victory moved the Hawks into a first-place tie with Boston, setting up the drive toward the Prince of Wales Trophy in the final week.

The 15 shutouts by Esposito were more remarkable than the 13 by Lumley in other ways than just the margin of two more. Esposito achieved his shutouts in 63 games played. Lumley played in 69. But Coach Reay made another point:

"I never thought I'd see the day that record would be broken. Not with the kind of hockey that's played today and with the slapshot being used. There's no doubt in my mind that players—on the average—shoot harder than they did 15 or 20 years ago. We had a few men who could drive the puck, sure, but not as many as today with the slapshot. And a goalkeeper has to play a little more protectively than he had to years ago. That puck's winging at him. The strain is much greater than it used to be, and he takes more of a beating. What Esposito has done is incredible."

It really was incredible, and the newspapers started calling him "Tony Zero," a most fitting nickname. Yet even the record of 15 shutouts doesn't tell the full story of what Esposito achieved. In 15 other games he gave up just one goal. In almost half of the 63 games in which he played, the opposition got one goal or less, an almost ironclad guarantee of victory to the Hawks.

How much of a strain this superb performance took out of Tony only he knows, and he won't tell. While the other Hawks were celebrating the clinching of first place after the wild 10-2 victory over Montreal on April 5, Tony sat limply in his locker room cubicle for almost 40 minutes. He smiled weakly and accepted a little champagne, then leaned back and stared again at the ceiling.

"Tired? I'm totally drained," he said slowly. "It's hard to believe what has happened. The pressure has been tremendous, but the way these guys played in front of me all season they deserved to win. They made it a lot easier for me—I owe them a great deal."

They owed *him* more and the debt increased a little. He went through the Stanley Cup quarterfinals with his skills undiminished, holding Detroit to two goals in each of the four games and giving the Hawks an unusual sweep with identical scores of 4-2.

It was only after the seven-day layoff between the Detroit series and the semifinals against Boston that he lost his edge. Even at that, who can say that the injury he suffered in the first minute of play in the opening game with the Bruins on April 19 at the Stadium didn't have something to do with that?

Boston's Ken Hodge took a slapshot from the corner at Tony's left and the puck hit the goalie directly over the left eye, stunning him and knocking him to the ice. It was a tremendous blow, and brother Phil, who saw it happen, could hardly keep from going to the Chicago cage.

"I didn't dare," said Phil, referring to the unwritten code of sports that separates even brothers by uniform. "But I was terribly worried. I immediately thought of how sick our goalie Eddie Johnston was after he took a similar shot in practice in a game with Detroit last year. I couldn't even go up to Tony. We don't speak to each other when we are playing and this is the play-offs."

While Hawk trainer Skip Thayer was working over Tony, Phil skated in circles at mid-ice, his head down.

"Finally, Bobby Orr and Bobby Hull came up and told me the kid was all right. I relaxed a little."

He didn't relax too much. He scored three of the first four Boston goals in a 6-3 Boston victory that started the Bruins off to their four-game sweep over the Hawks.

When the game was over, Tony manfully faced the reporters and refused to blame Hodge's stunning shot for his ineffectiveness that night. Even as he spoke, the imprint of the puck was visible over his left eye, although the shot had struck him on the mask.

"Hodge blasted it," said Tony. "I'm not blaming him —he was probably just hoping it would bounce off somebody into the net. It stunned me at the time, but it didn't affect my play at all. If I'd just come up with a couple of good saves we'd have won the game. I just played badly. There aren't any excuses."

There never were, not even after the final 5-4 defeat at Boston a week later, when the Bruins rained 54 shots on goal and Tony kept the Hawks in the game with some incredible saves. Time and again, the Hawk defense left him naked to his enemies, yet he refused to complain.

It was Phil, brother enemy, who finally spoke up: "They can't blame him for any of the goals. I know it doesn't sound right for me to back him and to knock his defense, but they didn't have it. They haven't had it. If it weren't for him they wouldn't have finished first. He put them there."

In the final summing up, neither would Reay blame Tony.

"How could I blame him? After what he has done for us this year how could I ever blame him? He brought us to the top. The main difference this year is the goalkeeping, the big save Tony has given us. Last year it was the bad goal that was beating us—they were getting by De Jordy. This year we've had Esposito making the big saves game after game, the save that gives you a lift. So many times you get that big save, and bang! You go right up to their end and put the puck in the net."

To the end Reay defended Esposito's style against critics, even though he himself at first had been worried by the flopping, diving way his curly-haired magician tends goal. Said Reay:

"He has got a great glove hand and he's hard to beat down low. It takes a shot into a high corner to beat him, and not too many guys can do that if the defense keeps them off balance. Some goalkeepers are a split second behind the play; Tony's a split second ahead of it. He may be awkward, but he's rarely out of position. You know, I get kind of tired of people knocking his style. He keeps the puck out, doesn't he?"

There is no arguing the answer to that question. Tony's 2.17 goals-against average earned the Vezina Trophy for the Hawks, and he also won the Calder Trophy as rookie of the year in the NHL. He was second only to Boston's Bobby Orr in the most valuable player voting.

He has come a long way from the game in 1968-69 when brother Phil scored those two goals on him and felt dreadful afterward: "I was worried for him before the game. I thought if he didn't do well he could be sent down. I thought I could ruin his career."

Only Tony himself, through sheer ineptitude, can ruin his career now. It is unlikely that will happen. Nobody ever would expect him to match his rookie season. He could play less ably and still be sensational.

Lou Angotti, awed by what he had watched at close range all season, discussed Tony's future when the 1969-70 play-offs ended:

"If Tony plays anywhere near as well next season as he did this year, no one in the league is going to be even close to him as a goalie. Certainly, he can't have the same kind of sensational year, but if he just has a real great year, he'll still be in a class by himself."

There is no reason why Tony can't keep up his fine play. He was 27 when the 1969-70 season ended and, according to Reay, most goaltenders mature later than other players. Tony is a well-conditioned athlete, and there's no touch of the flake in his personality. He's much more serious than his fun-loving brother Phil, who remarked: "Tony's the type of guy for whom 'hockey is hockey and business is business.' I respect him for it."

During his final college years Tony married a hometown girl, Marilyn, a beautiful, slender blonde whom he met at a dance while both were still in high school. Their son, Mark Anthony, was born while Tony was still playing at Vancouver. Marilyn attends every home game and responds emotionally to Tony's success—or failure.

"I do flinch every time there's a shot at Tony," she said. "I think I'm always whacking somebody near me without realizing it. And I hear what the fans are saying about him, even if they are critical. But I don't let that bother me. I figure they paid for their tickets and have a right to say what they want."

Like most athletes' wives, Marilyn finds there are drawbacks to being married to a celebrity.

"It's a lonely life in a way, with Tony on the road so much," she said. "You have to be a person who is able to manage on her own. But it's exciting at times and that more than compensates for the drawbacks."

She has learned to accept and understand her husband's moods.

"If he loses, he doesn't talk too much," she said. "He sort of goes over the game in his mind. If he wins, he starts thinking about the next game, so he's never really relaxed."

As serious as he is, Tony can be a fast man with a quip. Informed that colleague Gerry DesJardins, then playing for Los Angeles before moving to the Hawks, could move his hands from side to side at 118 m.p.h., Tony grinned.

"I could move my hands pretty fast, too, when somebody holds out a $100 bill to me," he joked.

His wit serves him well. He has been a radio announcer in Sault Ste. Marie during the off season and also has other profitable sidelines, such as instructing in a hockey school.

A newspaper advertisement for the school noted: "A limited number of goalies will be accepted. First registered will be taken." With Tony's record as a testimonial, the quota was filled almost instantly. It is highly unlikely that Mark Anthony will enroll in Tony's class in future years.

"I wouldn't mind if he became a hockey player," said Marilyn, "but I wouldn't want to have him become a goalie." Tony raised an eyebrow at that as if to say, "What's wrong with being a goalie." Come to think of it, nothing much if you're Tony Zero.

23

Maggie the Snowthrower

THERE is fire in his hair, for Keith Magnuson is crowned with a mop of red. But there is fire in his heart, too, and that's what makes him a great hockey player. He is a good one, a brave one, a devil on skates with the green eyes of a cat and the mien of an angel. And for the Black Hawks nothing like him had come along since Stan Mikita 11 years before.

Magnuson never had played a professional game before when he reported at training camp in September 1969. He was fresh out of Denver University and a defenseman, which made it even more unlikely that he could immediately achieve one of the more difficult feats in sports and break into the NHL as a regular.

It is difficult not only because of the skill involved but because hockey is a punishing game. It is a game that cuts, bruises, breaks, and frightens. It is a test of courage as much as of skill. Unless the two go hand-in-hand there is no room for a man. Says Coach Reay:

"There are two things you're looking for in a rookie when you first see him. Attitude is a big percentage, for wanting to play is a great thing in a guy's favor. That and intestinal fortitude. In some cases a guy will have a great deal of ability and he'll get by on it for a year or two. But it takes more than that in the long run. It takes a lot of guts to be a National Leaguer. There is bound to be bodily contact in this game, and you're going to be man-to-man sooner or later.

"In this game you're looking for 'snowthrowers,' guys who put on the brakes and aren't afraid to challenge a man or to handle anything that comes their way. They're going to have to pass the test, and nobody else can do it for them."

It is the way of the world on the ice and no one in such a brief time has been given more opportunity to prove his courage than Magnuson. From the start he had to use his fists almost as much as his stick. He rang up two dozen fights (three in one game, with Oakland's Carol Vadnais —breaking his opponent's nose) and led the NHL in penalty minutes with 213 as a rookie. He has said modestly:

"I really don't go looking for fights. I don't know how I get into them. Most of the time I guess it comes when you're trying to get a guy away from the front of the net. You just can't let them stand there. You might hit a fella in the head with your stick and he'll let you have it across the shins. If a fight comes up, it comes up and I'm there. Some of these guys are a little chippy though. You just touch them a little bit and they want to fight. Boston is very chippy. Maybe it's part of their image."

To protect himself in the clinches at all times, Magnuson has studied karate. He used to practice on walls and boards but now he just whistles his hands through the air every night.

"I knew they would be running at me my first year, testing me; so I took karate all summer. The only trouble is I can't use it that much. The secret is using your feet, and when your feet are in skates it's not exactly legal. I'm going to practice boxing and wrestling."

Reay was delighted from the start with the aggressiveness of the youngster. Before Magnuson arrived the Black Hawks were gaining a reputation as pigeons around the league. Said Reay, with great satisfaction:

"Magnuson getting in all these scrapes means he's doing something on the ice to irritate somebody else. I wouldn't put him in the category of being a mean player, but a player who is taking care of himself and who is doing his job. If you're not doing anything on the ice, you're not going to get into scrapes. The fact he is getting into these things is good. He gets tested throughout the league and he has got to pass the test."

As a rookie, Magnuson had a grade of "A." Nobody shoved him around in the finals of the series of tests he had to pass to get into the NHL. And most of what he has achieved has been his own doing. It has to be like that.

It started in the little town of Wadena, Saskatchewan, near Saskatoon. That's where Magnuson was born on April 27, 1947, and where he got his first pair of ice skates. He is the youngest by far of three sons of an insurance salesman, and from the beginning had to live up to the pace set by his elder brothers.

Some younger children buckle under that kind of competition and quit trying as hard as they might, because they are afraid they cannot equal the older members of their families. Others, like Keith, are motivated all the more. It may be that Keith's tremendous inner drive comes from what the psychologists term "sibling rivalry," the determination of a younger son to equal or excel his older brothers. Keith admitted it.

"Dale, who is 11 years older than me and a doctor, and Wayne, who is eight years older and a teacher, were fine hockey players when they were younger. They made quite a reputation for themselves in the leagues around town and even thought about being professionals. They gave me something to live up to as I grew older. I wanted to be as good as they were, and I guess it made me play that much harder. I didn't want to let them down."

Although he was the youngest, his brothers never treated him like a baby. They were as tough on him as they were on others or on themselves when it came to sports.

"They used to take me with them to play a little catch with a football. They didn't let up either. They threw the ball at me as hard as they could and as often as not knocked me to the ground. It was good for me. It made me hard."

It was a toughening of the spirit as well as of the body. There was no mercy for little Keith, not from his brothers. They didn't wipe his eyes or soothe his bruised feelings.

The pounding helped to make good football material out of Keith. He was a quarterback in high school. More important to his future, it also made a hockey player of him and instilled in him the desire to become a professional.

"It is all I ever wanted to be from the time I knew what being a pro meant. Nothing else has ever appealed to me. When I was 10 years old I'd go with my best friend, Tim Gould, to the rink after school. We'd stay there until they threw us out, sometimes until 1:00 in the morning. Our parents would worry about where we were."

Every Saturday night he would watch the telecasts of the Toronto Maple Leafs game. Frequently, he wrote to the Leafs players asking for autographed pictures. He also wrote to Gordie Howe of Detroit, who sent back a photograph signed, "Good luck and best wishes to my friend Keith." And he began learning how to play hockey.

"I went through the usual gradations of the hockey leagues, the Pee Wee, Bantams, and so on, but there wasn't really an opportunity to play advanced hockey in our area because the teams weren't good enough. And my dad insisted I get an education."

Both parents had a drive for education. Keith's father, Joe, had been denied an opportunity to continue schooling in his youth. Rather than permit Keith to play in the higher amateur leagues, the principal training grounds for pros, he insisted that the boy go to college.

"He was a farm boy, and he had no opportunity to go to college. Yet he worked himself up. But he wanted to make

sure his children got an education. He insisted Dale become a doctor and was happy when Wayne became a
teacher. He wanted me to do as well."

As much as Keith's parents appreciated his love of
sports, they also wanted him to have something in life
besides trophies and bruises.

"Ever since I was a kid my mom wanted to get me interested in music. She wanted me to play the piano. I
even took some lessons on the trumpet, too, but all I ever
wanted to think about was sports."

While he was in grade school his mother got him started
as a stamp collector. His collection now numbers somewhere around 15,000.

Dad Magnuson and Keith finally arrived at a solution
that perfectly combined education and the desire to pursue
a hockey career. Keith could have attended a Canadian
university where hockey is subordinated completely to
learning. Instead, he was able to get a scholarship to Denver University, which provides a fine education but also
places great emphasis on hockey as an intercollegiate
sport. Coach Murray Armstrong, a former pro, has developed several U.S. national championship teams at
Denver, recruiting the players chiefly from Canada. Keith
says:

"It really couldn't have been a better setup. I could
combine getting an education with playing hockey. I considered my college as part of training for the pros. Coach
Armstrong made me get used to working, to practicing
fundamentals over and over again. We got three hours
of practice every day and played a 36-game schedule. I
think the habit of practicing regularly and for long periods
was as important as the games played. I was lucky enough
to play four years and get in all the extra practice."

He didn't neglect his education or his future off the ice
either. He earned a degree in business administration and
spent the summer of 1969 in a training program with a
Denver real estate company. Not that his mind was al-

together on real estate. He already was looking forward to getting a chance to make the Black Hawks.

Just to make sure he'd make the most of that chance, Keith got together with Cliff Koroll and Jim Wiste, who had left Denver to start their pro careers at Dallas the previous season, and worked out with them every day. He knew there is a big difference between college hockey and that in the NHL. He practiced skating three times a week and built up his legs by interminably running up and down the steps at the Denver Universty football Stadium. And he even worked with weights to strengthen his shoulders as well as taking karate lessons three times a week.

When September arrived, Keith reported to the Hawks' training camp at the Stadium. For a time Ivan and Reay concealed their enthusiasm, but after Magnuson and his agent were safely signed to a contract, the coach and general manager started warbling the boy's praises.

Ivan sat in the stands during a workout one day soon after Magnuson had signed his contract and his eyes sparkled as he watched the boy. And then Ivan commented:

"He's a helluva prospect, I'm not saying he's going to be a great player or a super star, or anything like that, but he has the potential. What makes him that good a prospect? His desire. He wants to play, he's eager to play, he's willing to play. He's aggressive. He's mobile. If you have those three things, you don't need anything more."

Coming from the man who had developed Gordie Howe and Bobby Hull and who has seen countless other great, good, and ordinary players come and go, the words were strong. Ivan caught himself, and smiled.

"You can get fooled. There are some rookies that have tremendous first years, then tail off the second year and are just ordinary. I've seen it so often. But this boy gives every indication of becoming a fine player."

Reay was as enthusiastic as Ivan about Keith and it was

evident from his facial expression that his words were genuinely meant:

"I'd never seen the youngster but I'd gotten good reports on him. He has lived up to them. I am impressed with his skating, of course, but what has impressed me even more is his willingness."

There was no question in the minds of Ivan and Reay; Keith was ready to play in the NHL. It was quite a feat for a defenseman, jumping from college hockey to the big league, and if Reay was pleasantly shocked, Keith was delighted— though not altogether surprised.

"I hate to ever sound conceited," Keith said, "but I thought I could make the club. I wouldn't have settled for Dallas (the Hawks' farm team). I wanted to make Chicago so bad I could taste it."

He was quick to correct any erroneous impression that he considered himself a polished player.

"You never stop learning in this game," he said. "I have to work on my shot and my passing, and I have to settle on a stick I like. I've got to learn to skate without looking at the puck. I've got to become instinctive about making the right play."

It is this continuing desire in Keith to improve himself that has so impressed Reay, who said:

"You never can be sure that a kid coming out of college is really serious about becoming a professional hockey player. But Keith is as determined as anybody I've ever seen to play in the National League. He has shown me a terrific amount of desire and ability to play defense."

Reay, plagued for years by defensemen who forgot their primary task—playing defense, was captivated in particular by one aspect of Keith's attitude. He remarked:

"It's not unusual for a defenseman to come into the league at 22, but it *is* unusual for a rookie to play defensively and be defense-minded. Most players—even defensemen—grade themselves on offense. When you talk to them, that's the impression you get. But this boy is

different. He plays DEFENSE. He is seldom out of position. If he makes a mistake it is because of lack of experience, not because he's being offense-minded."

Keith confirmed Reay's impression that defensive play
comes first in his mind.

"I don't care if I don't score goals. What I'm concerned
about is not having any goals scored against us while I'm
on the ice. And I like checking. What I like best about
hockey is the physical contact. I like to take a guy into the
boards, to set up a good pass."

As much as anything else, Keith's willingness to pound
the opposition, to take a man out with a solid check or to
return punch for punch, has endeared him to Reay. This
willingness to "mix" and his defense-mindedness eased
his way as a regular despite a few shortcomings his first
season.

"He has to work on his shooting and skating," said Reay.
"He has to smooth it off and take off a little better. But
I'm not about to complain. We were kissed by the angels
when we got this boy."

It took Magnuson only a few games to prove himself as
far as Ivan was concerned—and without the Hawks winning any of them. They dropped their first five games of the
1969-70 season, and when they managed to tie New York
1-1 in the sixth Ivan was bubbling with enthusiasm—not
about the game, but about Magnuson's conduct, declaring:

"The kid was the most impressive boy on the ice. He
started right off from the opening whistle and played consistently well. He plays for keeps and nobody pushes him
around. When he got the misconduct penalty (late in the
game with the score already tied 1-1) I was worried about
the effect because he had been playing so well and we
might miss him. This boy is going to be a fine player if he
plays at all up to what he has shown already."

Keith not only played up to his early showing, but continued to improve steadily as the Hawks began to right

themselves and started the climb to the top. His battering style of play and his willingness to throw punches quickly made him the darling of the fans in the Stadium. He quickly built up feuds with Boston's Derek Sanderson, Oakland's Carol Vadnais, Pittsburgh's Glenn Sather, and other similarly combative men.

For one stretch Manguson was involved in a fight in every game but disclaimed any particular fondness for fisticuffs, almost deploring the need for such unseemly behavior. He has said:

"Fighting shouldn't be part of hockey at all, but if you don't fight back in this game they'll run all over you. Besides, if you let the other team know you're around it lifts your team, it can fire them up."

That's just what Magnuson did, as the Hawks really began to start winning in early January. He fired them up. He helped make them aggressive, combative, and respected. His pugnacity indirectly helped to produce goals as opposing teams were more hesitant to pick on the Hawk forwards knowing that Magnuson was ready to throw off his gloves.

"We have some of the smaller forwards in the league," said Keith. "I don't like to see them being pushed around, and I feel it's my business to move in and help them out of trouble."

He was always moving in. One of the more protracted battles of the season was with Pittsburgh's Sather in a game on January 14 at the Stadium, Sather and Magnuson fighting both in the second and third periods. The first scrap was touched off when Sather jumped Mikita from behind in the second period and dumped him to the ice. Magnuson was on the scene instantly.

"When he jumped on Stan I started pulling him off," said Keith later. "He said, 'Is that all you can do, jump on a guy from behind?' so I said 'You can go you know where,' and that started it."

The linesmen quickly separated the combatants, but while they were holding them, Sather flung his gloves, one after the other, at Magnuson.

"I thought it was sort of bush to throw his gloves at me," said Keith. "That didn't make me mad, but then he said something and I wanted to get at him."

Late in the third period, Sather tickled Magnuson in the rib with his stick, and that set off another round of brawling.

After the game, a 5-0 victory for the Hawks and Esposito's ninth shutout, Magnuson again set forth his principles of conduct on ice:

"Anyplace is the right place to fight if you've got a reason. Sather gave me plenty of reason. Besides, I think we can win a lot of games if we don't let the other guys knock us around. It's like skating, shooting, and checking. And it has to be a team effort. If one guy does it, the whole team does."

The Hawks' continuing success as they climbed out of fifth and started hurtling their way past the leaders in early March seemed to confirm his view. Coach Reay became more and more impressed with him:

"He's a very heady player, considering his age. He has been very hard to move out of there when he gets in front of that net. He has the wide-legged stance—it looks like he has been riding horses—that gives him great stability."

The "stability" his bow-legged stance provided wasn't always enough to save Magnuson from embarrassment. In November, in the first game between the Hawks and Detroit, he dropped his gloves to take a shot at Gordie Howe, his childhood idol. It was almost an act of sacrilege; most young players are too awed by Howe to do more than smile weakly as he gently nudges them with an elbow or raps them across the nose with his stick. The older ones know he'll choose his moment to retaliate for any affront to his venerable dignity, even if it takes months for the opportunity to arise. On March 26, at Detroit, Howe found the chance to repay Keith. He caught Magnuson looking elsewhere and jerked his feet out from under him—to the delight of the Detroit crowd. "He's a tough kid, but he'll learn," Howe muttered to Doug Jarrett, as he skated majestically away.

He learned well enough. The Hawks won that March 26 game 1-0 to give Esposito his record-setting 14th shutout, and maintained the pressure on Boston in the race for first place. It was the kind of game Magnuson admittedly never had experienced before. As he sat limply in the locker room thinking about the new sensations he had undergone; he said:

"Usually I'm one of the first to congratulate Tony, but tonight I was one of the last. I was just limp. The pressure of that game was unbelievable. I kept seeing Howe tying us in the last 30 seconds the way he beat us once earlier in the year. Pressure like this—I'm not used to it."

He really wasn't, yet he held up remarkably well as the Hawks roared on to the victory over Montreal that gave them first place on the final day of the regular season. He even curbed his natural aggressiveness in keeping with Reay's warning toward the end not to take unnecessary penalties.

"I get mad out there and I'm not afraid to fight anyone," said Keith, "but we've come too far for one individual to louse things up now."

He didn't do that at any point and played magnificently in the four-game sweep over Detroit in the Stanley Cup quarterfinals. And even against Boston, during the disastrous four games of the semifinals, Magnuson stood out, if not always for making the right play, always for his tremendous determination.

In the final game, with the score 2-0 in Boston's favor early in the second period, Keith blasted a shot from right point that went past Cheevers to get the Hawks back into contention. He had gone 83 games as a professional without scoring a goal—the 76 games of the regular season, the four games with Detroit, and the first three with Boston. Now, in a desperate moment he had put in the first goal of his career. It was to no avail in the final accounting, as the Hawks lost what proved to be a desperate struggle, too. So Keith couldn't feel gratified.

In the locker room he shook off the praise from well-wishers concerning his fine play. "But we didn't win!" he kept protesting. Then he went on:

"We didn't get a break in the whole series, not one. Still, we learned a lot, at least we younger players did. We learned about play-off hockey, how different it is from the regular season, how much more pressure there is. We sat around a week after the Detroit series listening to everybody telling us how great we were. We had finished first, and the Detroit series went boom-boom-boom-boom—four games in a row—and we didn't learn about playoffs. Then we came up against a tough opponent, and the younger players learned a lot, that play-off hockey is different."

They did, especially Magnuson, and Boston's Ken Hodge, even in the flush of victory, found kind words for his redheaded young foe:

"That Magnuson is going to be a helluva hockey player with all the determination he has got. I noticed he was the first guy on the ice and the first guy off it. And when he was on he worked. He and Koroll were the only guys Chicago had out there who were willing to mix it."

The tribute was sincere and Hodge's judgment of Magnuson's future is fully in keeping with that of Ivan and Reay. They know there are some rough edges in Magnuson's play but are certain there is no limit to his willingness to improve.

It was clear after the 1969-70 season that Magnuson, like most rookies, had "made" the league without quite completing his climb into the front ranks of stars. A rookie or young player is always on trial, no matter how good he might be or seem at first glance. That's because the first impression is more concerned with what a young fellow is going to be able to do someday than with what he has achieved at the moment.

Ivan's careful words describe Magnuson as having unlimited "potential." Note the word "potential." In Ivan's vocabulary that means he has the ability to achieve whatever he wants to if he is determined to do so.

There is no reason to think he isn't.

24

End of the Beginning

THE PAGE is turned. Although the age of Stan Mikita and Bobby Hull is not past, the Black Hawks venture deeper into the 1970's with the "new look" of a fresh decade already upon them.

With the end of the 1969-70 season they left behind—in a sense—their old rivals by moving into the Western Division of the NHL, to join Oakland, Minneapolis, Los Angeles, St. Louis, Pittsburgh, and Philadelphia. No longer will their confrontations with Montreal, Boston, New York, Toronto, and Detroit have the urgency of the past until they meet in the Stanley Cup play-offs.

Chances are the Hawks will prosper in their new setting and possibly even dominate the Western Division for years to come—if they retain the hunger and willingness to work that characterized them in 1969-70. As Stan Mikita warns:

"The greatest danger is that we'll think that all we have to do is show up in the Western Division and that we'll rip right through it. We've got to play just the way we did in finishing first. If we do that, we'll be all right. We've got a lot of good young kids and they should be that much better as they add experience."

Ken Hodge of the Stanley Cup champion Boston Bruins viewed the rival Hawks in the same light:

"They're at the same stage we were a couple of years ago. They've got a lot of good young players and some veterans at their peak. They're going to keep getting better, and they're not going to be easy to beat a couple of years from now."

Bobby Hull was just 31 at the end of the 1969-70 season. He scored 38 goals in just 61 games despite his greater concentration on defensive play, and there is no reason to think that there aren't some more 50-goal seasons in his future.

Mikita turned 30 and despite an aching back came up with 39 goals and 47 assists for 86 points. Billy Reay regarded it as Stan's finest season, and the great center should have even better ones ahead.

Pit Martin, just 26, had his best scoring year with 30 goals and 33 assists for 63 points. His linemate, Jim Pappin, 30, came up with 28 goals and 25 assists for 53 points. In the stretch drive for first it was Pappin and Martin who came up with the big goals, game after game.

Dennis Hull, 25, played much of the season with an emphasis on defense but managed to come up with 17 goals and 35 assists. "Nobody worked any harder than Dennis," said Reay. "It's too easy to overlook what he contributed to the team because it doesn't show in goals. But he was outstanding defensively."

These are the young veteran forwards, and on defense the story is much the same. Captain Stapleton is just 30 and figures on having five or six fine seasons ahead of him. Doug Jarrett, a six-year veteran at 26, turned around after a couple of mediocre seasons to play up to expectations in 1969-70. Bill White, 31, gave the Hawks a solid defensive reinforcement after the shock of Stapleton's injury.

These men are the core of the Hawks of the near future, the veterans who have proved themselves and who have many good seasons still ahead. And then there are the youngsters, the rookies who came along in 1969-70 to add the zest and spirit and surprisingly fine play that lifted a team from sixth place to first in one of the great turnabouts of all sports history.

First of all there's Tony Esposito the goaltender, winner of the Calder Trophy as NHL rookie of the year, second to Bobby Orr of Boston in the Most Valuable Player voting and the All-Star selection at his position. (Brother Phil of Boston also was selected to the All-Star team. It was the first time brothers had been selected together to the All-Star first team since goalie Tiny Thompson of the Bruins and left wing Paul Thompson of the Hawks were chosen in 1937-38.) Bobby Hull was chosen as left wing on the first team and Mikita as center on the second team.

Tony Zero at 27 is clearly just at the beginning of a fine career. He may never match his work in 1969-70 but— as Angotti noted—he could move down a notch and still be a great goaltender.

Behind Esposito the Hawks have Gerry Desjardins, just 26, with two seasons of NHL experience behind him. He tended goal in only four games of the 21 the Hawks played after acquiring him in February 1970. He played well and the Hawks won all four. Highly regarded by Reay, he is likely to relieve Esposito much more in the future.

If Esposito hadn't won the Calder Trophy, there is little question that it would have gone to Magnuson. At 23 the redhead is at the start of a career that Reay expects will place him with the great defensemen of hockey history.

Cliff Koroll, 24, and Gerry Pinder, 22, established themselves as solid NHL wings in their first season. Koroll scored 18 goals and 19 assists, while Pinder came up with 19 goals and 20 assists.

Reay was delighted with Koroll but excited by Pinder, who performed so well despite being on his off-side at left wing. (Pinder is normally a right wing, but the Hawks were short of left wings in 1969-70.)

"There's no telling how good he can become," said Reay. "He has got 'puck sense,' something you don't find often, the ability to be instinctively in the right spot at the right time."

Pinder also has something else—the brashness that often characterizes exceptional players and conviction that he is a good player. He wasn't tongue-tied, even as a rookie. He says what he thinks, and after getting a chance to play last season he popped off:

"It's about time I got on the ice. I was just about convinced I was glued to the bench. I don't want to be known as a guy who comes off the bench, but as a guy who prefers to play full time and can do it."

Coach Reay took the implied criticism in good part, saying:

"It didn't pass over my head. He hasn't complained to me and he'd better not. Gerry's a great prospect, a good skater, deceptively fast, and he has got good hockey instincts. But he's young and has a lot to learn. He'll get his chance to play."

Pinder did get his chance and proved himself. He also proved that spirit and zest can carry a young player and a team a long way in hockey. It was the story of the Hawks of 1969-70.

Now that the page is turned, a new challenge awaits this team whose story started with Major McLaughlin in 1926. After 44 years of effort the Black Hawks have yet to accomplish the triumph of finishing first and winning the Stanley Cup in the same year.

As overjoyed as Coach Reay was in leading the Hawks to their unexpected triumph of 1969-70, his career goal is unfulfilled.

"I've never coached a Stanley Cup champion yet," he said, almost wistfully. It is something to work toward— and he will, because he knows that it is only through hard work that it can be attained.

It is what the Hawks will be shooting for in the 1970's.

Season	W	L	T	F	Play-off Results	Top Goal Scorer	Goals
1926-27	19	22	3	3	Lost quarterfinal	Babe Dye	25
1927-28	7	34	3	3	Out of play-offs	Mickey Mackay	17
1928-29	7	29	8	5	Out of play-offs	Vic Ripley	11
1929-30	21	18	5	2	Lost quarterfinal	John Gottselig	21
1930-31	24	17	3	2	Lost final	John Gottselig	20
1931-32	18	19	11	2	Lost quarterfinal	John Gottselig	13
1932-33	16	20	12	4	Out of play-offs	Paul Thompson	13
1933-34	20	17	11	2	Won Stanley Cup	Paul Thompson	20
1934-35	26	17	5	2	Lost quarterfinal	John Gottselig	19
1935-36	21	19	8	3	Lost quarterfinal	Paul Thompson	17
1936-37	14	27	7	4	Out of play-offs	Paul Thompson	17
1937-38	14	25	9	3	Won Stanley Cup	Paul Thompson	22
1938-39	12	28	8	7	Out of play-offs	John Gottselig	16
1939-40	23	19	6	4	Lost quarterfinal	Cully Dahlstrom	11
1940-41	16	25	7	5	Lost semifinal	George Allen	14
1941-42	22	23	3	4	Lost quarterfinal	Red Hamill	24
1942-43	17	18	15	5	Out of play-offs	Doug Bentley	*33
1943-44	22	23	5	4	Lost final	Doug Bentley	*38
1944-45	13	30	7	5	Out of play-offs	Bill Mosienko	28
1945-46	23	20	7	3	Lost semifinal	Max Bentley	31
1946-47	19	37	4	6	Out of play-offs	Max Bentley	29

SEASON	W	L	T	F	PLAY-OFF RESULTS	TOP GOAL SCORER	GOALS
1947-48	20	34	6	6	Out of play-offs	Gaye Stewart	27
1948-49	21	31	8	5	Out of play-offs	Roy Conacher	26
1949-50	22	38	10	6	Out of play-offs	Metro Prystal	29
1950-51	13	47	10	6	Out of play-offs	Roy Conacher	26
1951-52	17	44	9	6	Out of play-offs	Bill Mosienko	31
1952-53	27	28	15	4	Lost semifinal	Jim McFadden	23
1953-54	12	51	7	6	Out of play-offs	Pete Conacher	19
1954-55	13	40	17	6	Out of play-offs	Ed Litzenberger	23
1955-56	19	39	12	6	Out of play-offs	John Wilson	24
1956-57	16	39	15	6	Out of play-offs	Ed Litzenberger	32
1957-58	24	39	7	5	Out of play-offs	Ed Litzenberger	32
1958-59	28	29	13	3	Lost semifinal	Ed Litzenberger	33
1959-60	28	29	13	3	Lost semifinal	Bobby Hull	*39
1960-61	29	24	17	3	Won Stanley Cup	Bobby Hull	31
1961-62	31	26	13	3	Lost final	Bobby Hull	*50
1962-63	32	21	17	2	Lost semifinal	Bobby Hull and Stan Mikita	31
1963-64	36	22	12	2	Lost semifinal	Bobby Hull	*43
1964-65	34	28	8	3	Lost final	Bobby Hull	39
1965-66	37	25	8	2	Lost semifinal	Bobby Hull	*54
1966-67	41	17	12	1	Lost semifinal	Bobby Hull	*52
1967-68	32	26	16	4	Lost semifinal	Bobby Hull	*44
1968-69	34	33	9	6	Out of play-offs	Bobby Hull	*58
1969-70	45	22	9	1	Lost semifinal	Stan Mikita	39

KEY: W—Won. L—Lost. T—Tied. F—position in standings. *—Led league.